THIS UNSUCCESSFUL AGE

THIS
UNSUCCESSFUL AGE

or

The Pains of Economic Progress

by

WALTER EUCKEN

Late Professor of Economics, Freiburg University

With an Introduction by

JOHN JEWKES, C.B.E.

Professor of Economic Organisation, University of Oxford

New York
OXFORD UNIVERSITY PRESS
1952

MADE AND PRINTED IN GREAT BRITAIN BY
MORRISON AND GIBB LIMITED, EDINBURGH AND LONDON

CONTENTS

INTRODUCTION

I

I FIRST met Walter Eucken at the foundation conference of the Mont Pèlerin Society at Vevey in 1948. His appearance there aroused no little interest. At the time a civilian traveller across the border from the chaos that was Germany was a rarity. But Eucken had, in any case, already become something of a legend among liberal economists. I imagine that few British-born economists knew much of his pre-war work, although even then the rumours had spread of his growing influence among the younger German liberals. The really arresting fact about him, however, was that he was still alive. He had remained in Germany throughout the war, steadfastly adhering to liberal principles which must have been anathema to the Hitler regime. It was known that he had endured much. Yet he had survived and apparently still retained sufficient energy and resiliency to take his part actively with other liberal economists from all over the world in an attempt to reformulate the principles out of which, to use a favourite phrase of Eucken's, "modern industrialized society could be organized in a humane and efficient way."

His presence added much to the memorable quality of that first conference. He looked a great man. He was tall and commanding and of a countenance which, although shrunken into stark lines by suffering and pity, still retained its kindliness and the serenity of an undeviating integrity. He modestly intervened in discussions, analyzing the utter breakdown of co-operative economic effort in Germany as a consequence of complete central planning and speculating upon human societies with a wisdom distilled from great historical knowledge and his gift for powerful and penetrating

7

analysis.   Here was a fine flowering of European
learning, seeming the brighter because it was occurring
in an age when shallow and arrogant intellectualism
had unleashed most of the evils of which men are
capable.

It was doubtless this rare combination of character
and learning which brought to Eucken after the war a
burden of work too great for any one man, which contributed to his final exhaustion and led to his untimely
and tragic death.   But he did not labour without result.
The published works in which he drew on German
experience for his conclusions concerning the pre-
requisites of ordered society command increasing respect.
And the advice he was able to give to his own government undoubtedly help to explain why Germany, of all
countries in Europe, has most clearly understood and
most firmly rejected the evils of central state planning
and has, through the establishment of sound currency
and free enterprise, provided one of the most remarkable cases of the swift restoration of a dislocated society.

In this present essay, which was intended as a course
of lectures at the London School of Economics, Eucken
set out to summarize, and perhaps popularize, his main
ideas whilst adding to them some deductions based on
very recent experience in Germany.   Writing before the
events in Korea threw the world again into turmoil,
he obviously considered the time ripe to press upon as
wide an audience as possible his crucial question :
" How can the modern industrialized economy and
society be organized in a humane and efficient way ? "
The question was opportune for two reasons.   First,
because the people of Europe had completely lost faith
in *laissez-faire* and had, in five short years since the war,
also become disenchanted with the centrally planned
economy.   There was, therefore, a vacuum which would
undoubtedly be quickly filled either with ideas offering
some hope of a stable society or with some new set of
social fallacies from among the innumerable perversions

of which the human mind can be prey. Second, because since 1900 there has been much experience of a very wide range of social and economic organisations. In the first half of this century Europe has picked up and tossed out one system after another, like children scrabbling in a lumber room. So that, if social scientists are really concerned about the relative merits, in fostering justice and guaranteeing continuity, of different forms of society, and if economic science has any relevance in providing such assessments, the material for study and analysis is there to hand.

Eucken's essay is so short and so fluently presented that it would be presumptuous to strive for further compression or re-wording. But I think it is relevant to point out that this brief work reveals his outstanding characteristics of integrity and courage. There are too many recent liberal tracts which calmly ignore what has happened in the world in the last quarter of a century and continue to gloss over the fundamental, and still largely unresolved, dilemmas of a liberal society. Eucken, on the other hand, pushes his reader hard against these very problems ; indeed the essay may be said to be written around them. There is, first, the problem that, whilst a liberal economy must be based on freedom of contract, that very freedom may be used by business men to create monopolies which are a negation of freedom of contract. " The principle of freedom of contract thus comes into open conflict with the competitive principle." There is, second, the dilemma that whilst society must confer upon the state *some* authority and power, " the possession of power provokes arbitrary action, endangers the freedom of other people and destroys mature and good institutions." There is, third, the possibility that a competitive society, whatever its other merits, may deprive us of the full economies of large-scale industrial operation. And there is finally the sombre dilemma, as Eucken sees it, that whilst mass unemployment is repugnant to the social conscience, a policy of full employment leads directly, *via* inflation, to a centrally planned, and therefore totalitarian, society.

It is the virtue of the essay that it goes far in providing rational solutions of these dilemmas. But in one case, that of the treatment of full employment, Eucken is, to my mind, less convincing than elsewhere. This is a matter on which an English liberal frequently finds himself at variance with his confrères on the Continent and in America and which, therefore, merits an examination of the issues between them.

Whence arises Eucken's distrust of state policies for maintaining full employment? If, at a time when unemployment appears to be higher than can be explained by seasonal influences or the normal decay of older industries, the government comes in with such measures as budget deficits and public works, an expansion of employment may be expected. That, however, is only the first, and the favourable, consequence of a long chain of reactions the later links of which are likely to be highly unfavourable. The accepted methods of maintaining full employment, by increasing the stream of money, will cause or will threaten inflation. The government cannot be indifferent to the rise in prices consequential upon its own actions. If it were, then the rise in prices would lead to demands for increased wages and an open and continuous inflation would result. The government will wish to check the price increase by imposing price controls. To impose price controls is tantamount to discarding the price system as the method of distributing resources ; for at the fixed prices demand will be greater than supply. It becomes necessary, therefore, to substitute a system of state allocation of goods for the now virtually discarded system of distribution through prices. The state has then embarked upon a course which has no logical end save a completely centrally planned economy. One special, and to Eucken particularly dangerous, form of state control arises through the disturbance of the balance of payments. The inflation creates a surplus of imports which normally might be expected to produce a change in the external value of money. If, whilst seeking to maintain other prices stable, the government believes it important to maintain a stable exchange rate, then imports too must be rationed. And the rationing of imports implies control over the whole economic system. In this diagnosis, full employment leads to central planning and a totalitarian society *via* repressed inflation.

There is much evidence, both of fact and of theory, to support such a line of reasoning, much more indeed than Eucken assembles in this short essay where he relies upon German experience alone. Such a chain of events occurred in Germany after 1933. Since 1945, in every country which has committed itself to a full employment policy, these three conditions have been found in close association : full employment, inflation, and the constant pressure upon the government to impose further and positive directions upon an economy which seems sluggishly incapable of adjusting itself to changing economic needs. History, therefore, supports the conclusion that full employment reached by the now popular methods paves the way for a regimented society.

The reasoning is undoubtedly fortified by considering the circumstances which will normally surround the operation of a full employment policy. What Eucken fears has not only happened in the past, it is also likely to happen in the future. Governments are often weak and self-seeking. Ministers are, in the nature of things, more subject to the defects of character fostered by the possession of power and, therefore, whatever may be their natural dispositions, more liable to self-deception than others. It is politically of great advantage for them to be able to claim that they have been responsible for maintaining full employment. They may be unaware of the causal link between the measures they adopt to maintain employment and the steps to which they are constantly and progressively driven in imposing further controls on the public.   Even where they are conscious of the consequences of their own acts they can gain a double political benefit by claiming first that they are keeping the community at work and, further, that they are enforcing, by controls and allocations, a fair and economic distribution of the goods and services in short supply—although, indeed, these shortages are directly attributable to their own actions.   In a Minister who favours controls and allocations on doctrinaire grounds, the realization that full employment implies controls carries with it no great terrors.   He will be the less inclined, therefore, to take pains to prevent his full employment measures from damaging a healthy currency.   To this argument Eucken, in his essay, contributes a further point which I think is new and is, in any case, extremely important.   A surplus of money helps to create an appearance of success for a centrally planned economy.   For so long as there is excessive purchasing power whatever is produced can be sold, the errors of the planners are buried by the omnivorous demand.   It is a scarcity of money which " explodes the planned economy," which restores the power of choice of the consumer and thereby reveals the wrong proportions in which goods are being produced.   To sum up : so far the governments which have most actively favoured full employment policies are not likely to be deterred by the inflation and the necessity for controls which can so easily follow.

It must be further accepted that even those of ingrained liberal instincts would find it extremely difficult to pursue a full employment policy without, at times, making mistakes the price of which would be inflation. There is no space here to enlarge upon these technical difficulties, but they may be summarized. There is, first, the unsolved, and indeed to my mind the scientifically insoluble, question of what level of employment constitutes full employment. No one can determine what part of existing unemployment is unconnected with a general deficiency in demand. Such elements as seasonal unemployment can be assessed in the light of the experience of the past. But how can the degree of structural unemployment be assessed ? Past experience there is useless. What is required is prediction, a forecast of the future course of individual industries. And economic predictions have a way of going wrong. So long as there is uncertainty regarding the existing scale of structural unemployment, this unemployment is likely to be underestimated and the budget deficits pushed beyond the proper point. The second technical difficulty is also bound up with the hazards of prediction. Full employment policy has come to be associated with economic tables, prepared annually, designed to indicate whether in the coming year total demand, as represented by total consumption plus total investment, will be sufficient to maintain the defined volume of full employment. The two crucial items in the preparation of such tables are the productivity of labour and the volume of investment likely to be carried through in the absence of exceptional state action. Any small error in the estimates here will produce a considerable falsification in the indicator as to the appropriate government policy. Estimates of labour productivity are hazardous, since no one even knows what are the variables of which productivity is a function. Errors in predicting " normal " investment and in basing appropriate remedial policy upon them are just as likely. Experience with the British Annual Economic Surveys makes the following points clear :

(1) The current volume of net investment is not, and cannot be, known except within very wide limits. The estimates presented of it represent residual figures of the differences between much larger elements, small errors in which would produce enormous errors in the residual.

(2) Estimates of future net investment are even more subject to error.

(3) The margins of error in the estimate of future investments are much too wide to provide guidance for policies aimed at maintaining employment within narrow margins, much less at a fixed point.

(4) In the absence of reliable units of measurement, the control of investment, even if the powers of control were perfect, would be very much a hit or miss matter. For the controlling agent might raise the rate of investment under the mistaken assumption that it was falling and *vice versa*.

(5) In Great Britain, despite attempts to impose control upon investment and despite the strategic position which the government holds in determining the investment in the nationalized industries, in housing and in private industry through allocation of raw materials, the evidence suggests that investment has risen when the controls were set to reduce it and fallen when the controls were set to increase it.

The conclusion must, I think, be that in anything which remotely resembles a free economy the measurements and predictions upon which full employment policy are based will be extremely crude and the controls imposed to enforce the policies suggested by these measurements highly uncertain in operation. It does not necessarily follow from this, of course, that inflation must be the normal consequence of a full employment policy. Deflation might just as easily be the product of the policy. But inflation may arise and since it is always difficult politically to cure inflation, for it involves wresting from the public their legitimate expectations, the danger of chronic inflation is clearly present.

It is now well understood that full employment, through its upward pressure in wages, may result in inflation by that route. If, at the existing wage rates, the demand for labour is greater than its supply there seems nothing to prevent a steady increase in wages calling for a parallel extension of controls to suppress the ensuing inflation. The suggestion, often made, that this danger can be averted by a "national wages policy" is a weak evasion of the real difficulties. For if a "national wages policy" simply means that the state would each year determine the increase to be permitted in the total wage bill, then more questions are raised than answered. What evidence is there that any state organisation has means for determining the correct percentage general increase in wages? Why should it be assumed that such an organisation would be immune from the influences of the time and would not be likely to reach decisions which are in themselves inflationary? If a state body fixes the permitted general increase, how is this to be distributed among the various trades and occupations? If the individual bargaining power of trade unions is not disturbed, what reason is there for assuming that the sum total of individual bargains will add up to the general permitted increase? If the state undertakes the fixing in detail of all wage rates, then a centrally planned economy has been established by another route. For the fixing of individual wage rates could only be attempted in any systematic fashion if it were geared to some plan comprehending the distribution of labour between different occupations which in turn would need to be based on a comprehensive plan of the goods which had to be produced.

So far all the evidence seems strongly in favour of Eucken's chain of events : full employment, repressed inflation and a centrally controlled economy. The recent writings of those in the opposing camp in effect add force to his contentions by evading them. A recent instance is a publication of the United Nations[1] written by five economists who unanimously recommend that full employment policies should be carried out both jointly and severally by the industrial countries

---

[1] *National and International Measures for Full Employment*, 1949. The authors were Professor J. M. Clark, Mr. N. Kaldor, Professor A. Smithies, Mr. P. Uri and Mr. E. R. Walker.

of the world : each country to pursue measures to maintain internal demand, the countries jointly to accept international schemes for the prevention of balance of payment problems that may incidentally arise. These writers express the belief that full employment measures are consistent with the operation of free economies :

" The measures recommended in the present report to sustain effective demand do not involve any basic change in the economic institutions of private enterprise countries."

What answers then do they provide to the doubts expressed in the preceding paragraphs ? Mainly unhelpful platitudes. They discuss inflation not in terms of the actual and ever present danger it has proved to be, but as if it were some remote theoretical possibility which could always be dealt with, if the occasion arose, by a conference.

" If there is an upward pressure in prices, resulting from attempts to increase wages substantially more than the rate of increase in productivity, it might be necessary for governments, jointly with labour unions and representatives of management, to take action so as to ensure that such wage increases as may be granted will not lead to an inflationary price spiral."

Although it is notorious that bottlenecks in production are the normal concomitant of suppressed inflation, indeed the purpose of the suppression is to try to release these blockages, they profess that

" Bottlenecks in the production structure are likely to arise only in times of large-scale and rapid changes in the structure of demand such as occur in connexion with the conversion of an economy from peace to war or from war to peace."

What of the problem of structural unemployment ? The authors treat the matter lightly :

" There has undoubtedly been a tendency in the past to exaggerate the quantitative importance of the minor causes of unemployment and to overlook the fact that the main reason why . . . workers displaced from their regular work remain unemployed is the lack of alternative employment opportunities, which in turn is due to a deficiency of demand. This was proved by British experience during the war when large-scale so-called 'structural' unemployment, which had previously been attributed mainly to lack of mobility of labour, melted away, leaving an acute labour shortage. Similarly, the large-scale 'transitional' unemployment that was expected in many countries after the war simply failed to materialize, because as people were displaced from war jobs they were immediately absorbed into other employment."

Such illustrations are surely irrelevant. For unemployment in Great Britain in war-time was absorbed by a combination of labour direction, wage increases of a highly inflationary kind, conscription which moved men from industry to the army and the patriotic zeal of a community. And in most countries the transitional unemployment was slight simply because inflation, of a kind intolerable in normal times, was revealing its inevitable consequences.

When the authors are confronted with a type of structural unemployment, that in export trades, which they cannot brush aside, then they take refuge in generalities :

"If exports fail to revive, so that there is evidence that the fall in exports of any particular industry is the result of a long-term downward trend in foreign demand, the government should consider making the necessary structural adjustments."

But how does one identify a long-term downward trend until a long term has elapsed? And how does the government make these structural adjustments, whatever they may be?

In discussing the right role of investment in full employment policy they regard the problem as being automatically solved in a Socialist state—as if Socialist states never deliberately pushed investment to the point

B

at which inflation was inevitable, or as if such states never made mistakes as to the maximum investment possible without inflation. In discussing investment under private enterprise they recommend that governments should collect " advance information " of the investment plans of private firms, but they have no comment to offer on the well-known dilemma that the investment plans of private firms are not fixed and immutable but are the most slippery figures to obtain, to keep up to date or to rely upon in periods of economic change, precisely the periods when they are needed.

II

Yet, despite Eucken's cogent reasoning and the way in which his intellectual opponents play into his hands, not a few English Liberal economists remain convinced that the state has a useful function to perform in the prevention of unemployment by accepting ideas and adopting methods which would go beyond those heretofore accepted as constituting the proper role of government. They still think that what Keynes had to say about the possibilities of a deficiency of general demand, even if not new (as has recently become the popular cry), was true and justified an extension of the field for state action ; that his diagnosis of mass unemployment before the war was substantially a correct one and that no other diagnosis is nearly so convincing ; that no other body of theory extant offers us in future as good a chance of preventing unemployment on a scale intolerable to civilized communities and destructive of political stability ; and that, perhaps subject to some such conditions as set out below, it need not be considered impossible that the state can perform its new functions whilst preserving both currency stability and free enterprise.

Before enlarging upon these views, however, one

point may be mentioned on which all liberals will surely
be agreed. Eucken wisely says in this essay that, in any
case, "full employment policy is not enough." By
that he means that the types of industrial monopoly
which before the war were encouraged or created by the
state in many countries were, in themselves, a source of
growing instability and that, where the supply of money
was completely bound up with the granting of credit,
other causes of instability were thereby intensified.
Liberals will continue to enlarge upon the evils of
monopoly and closely administered markets, and there
is much fruitful discussion going on as to possible
methods of restoring to money its effectiveness in its
traditional roles as a medium of exchange and a unit of
account. But I find it difficult to accept the view that,
when everything has been done which can be done in
these spheres, full employment can then be taken for
granted. It does not appear reasonable, for instance,
to assume that the depression in the United States after
1929, with its catastrophic decline in national income,
can be wholly or even largely explained in terms of the
monopoly elements in the economy or the defects of
the credit system.

Experience of full employment policies since 1945 has
been of so restricted a kind that deductions drawn from
it may not be generally valid. In nearly every case
since the end of the war the governments which have
pursued, or have thought they were pursuing, full employment policies have been Socialist governments, that
is to say governments which, simultaneously with their
anxiety to maintain employment, have been busily re-
distributing income (in itself inflationary) and in trying
to give practical meaning to their theory of the planned
economy. Further, the period following the war was
inevitably a period of inflation—in war time the public
must always be made to think that it will, after victory,
be richer than is really possible. It is not, therefore,
surprising that in the past five years full employment,

inflation and planning have been present together. But what we are seeking for is not mere association, but inevitable, or at least highly probable, causal connection. On the other hand, the United States may, I suppose, be said to have enjoyed full employment since 1945 although the government has not claimed the credit for this despite its tentative efforts to employ budgetary policy on the one occasion when a recession seemed imminent. But full employment in the United States did not lead to the controls and allocations of a centrally planned economy. That may in part have been due to the increased productivity which checked inflation, in part to the acceptance of price increases which might have been suppressed by a government of different political colour ; but it was also due, presumably, to the fact that the planning craze had not affected the American public to the degree found elsewhere.

Suppose, however, for a moment that a full employment policy could be tested out under a different set of conditions and that a government is in power—

(1) which is of strong liberal disposition, is aware of the virtues of free markets and private enterprise, is conscious of the evils of open inflation and understands what happens when inflation is suppressed by stifling the symptoms whilst leaving the causes untouched ;

(2) which recognizes that a price system only works if relative prices are allowed to change, and that a moderate change in the general price level need not be a cause for panic nor even reason why the whole of the wage-earning class should simultaneously make a demand for wage increases ;

(3) which is prepared to take a much less mechanical and perfectionist view of full employment policy than is usually taken. By that I mean that it would not be too ambitious about its policy. It would not attempt to keep unemployment below 5 per cent. or 6 per cent. (at least through financial devices). It

would not commit itself to any minimum unemployment figure, for this would necessarily depend upon a qualitative judgment of existing conditions. It would recognize that an economy can only be progressive, as a whole, if parts of it are constantly dying and being replaced by new industries so that some structural unemployment is normal ;

(4) which understands that, highly desirable as it might be, accurate economic prediction is impossible and all schemes based upon other assumptions are likely to do more harm than good. This means that the government whilst, of course, collecting all relevant past information which may have some bearing on the future, would place no great reliance on the economic tables which purport to show how, in the future, aggregate demand can be brought to the appropriate level and what steps should be taken to bring about the balance for the future. The government would be prepared to act largely on the event ; it would consider that unemployment was likely to rise when it was beginning to rise. It would depend, for the effectiveness of its policy, more upon the *speed* of introducing its measures rather than upon its power to anticipate what should be done long before it needs to be done.

(5) which was prepared, when it did make mistakes in an inflationary direction, to accept some general price increases, including increases in the price of foreign money, and not try to put these mistakes out of sight by price control.

Let it further be assumed that the trade unions are guided by men who recognize that caution in pressing for wage increases in a position of full employment is just as essential a part of the use of the full employment technique as is the adoption of non-conducting devices in the use of electricity ; and that the public is fully aware of the more obvious relations between price movements and wage movements. In brief, that the

average citizen shows, in economic matters, the kind of
common sense and communal wisdom revealed in the
working of any mature political democracy : reluctance
to press in full what may appear to him to be legitimate
demands ; sagacious understanding of the evil social
consequences of apparently innocuous individual acts
multiplied endlessly ; sobriety in perceiving that there
are always some inequities which can be remedied only
at a cost quite out of proportion to the gain.

If these conditions were satisfied, could it still be said
that the periodic use of budget deficits and associated
devices to prevent mass unemployment was so dangerous
a weapon that it should not be thought of ; that a
Keynesian policy of a high and stable level of employment was a short cut to a totalitarian state ?

The reply, of course, will immediately be made that
the assumptions are fanciful, that the conditions laid
down impossible of satisfaction.   That is to say, even if
the Keynesian diagnosis and prescription, as a *technique*,
were logical, it is still wrong to imagine that the proper
institutional surroundings could be provided for it.   In
particular, those who attack the Keynesian ideas stress
the unlikelihood that any government, except one which
is prepared to allow unemployment to run its natural
and unimpeded course, could be trusted to resist and
prevent inflation.   It is precisely this anxiety, certainly
not without foundation in history, which leads many
liberal economists to advocate automatic mechanisms
for the preservation of the value of money : the gold
standard, 100 per cent. money, commodity reserve
money, the linking of budget deficits to minimum rates
of employment and so on.   I have great sympathy with
the motives behind these ingenious schemes.   Some of
the ideas are extremely attractive in principle and seem
to have a high practicability.   It is, however, important
to keep in mind that so long as governments are en-
trusted with power and responsibility, no automatic
device will check a government which is bent upon

inflation for, in the last resort, it will dispense with the controlling device. There is no foolproof or knave-proof way of " writing the value of money into the Constitution." It is a much more complicated social problem than that.

It may be that, so long as importance is attached to individual freedom, a Socialist government is the wrong kind of government to operate a full employment policy. But need we go further than that ? Need we accept the view that, under no circumstances, even with increasing knowledge and sense of responsibility on the part of a government and informed watchfulness on the part of every section of public opinion, can a public repugnance of inflation be fostered ? Is it quite impossible that a community could establish, as one of its most tenacious traditions, the view that the maintenance of the value of its money in free markets is a test of its national probity and its international standing ?

Events in Great Britain since 1945 provide some relevant evidence on these matters. In Great Britain the character and the drawbacks of " suppressed inflation " were quickly understood.[1] There is no doubt that Sir Stafford Cripps and his advisors accepted that diagnosis and pursued courageously a long-period policy of reducing inflation and that the public generally, despite the unpleasant effects for them, broadly supported that policy. I do not doubt that Sir Stafford Cripps attained a large measure of success. To assert so much is not to approve of the general economic policy of the government of the time. Oddly enough, it often declared that the purpose of its anti-inflation policy was " to make the controls work " whereas, of course,

[1] Even those who consider that economists have little real influence in the world (and that most frequently not for good) and that economic science has little relevance to the real problems must recognize the swift and brilliant perception of " suppressed inflation " and its consequences by British economists. My own feeling is that the credit of precedence should go to Sir Hubert Henderson who, in a short article in the *Sunday Times* in February 1947, put precisely the ideas to which others had been groping and gave us a conception of a new kind of inflation so patently true that it became a part of our general thinking almost overnight.

the purpose of an anti-inflation policy should be to destroy the purpose of the controls and allow the price mechanism to work. And, of course, the policy pursued at the time of trying to keep *both* the domestic price level and the external value of sterling constant was bound to cause something to smash, as it ultimately did in the devaluation of 1949. But this does not alter the fact that a Minister did take sound advice, did pursue unpleasant policies courageously, and that the public, whilst grumbling, understood generally what was on foot and co-operated.

Further, in this same period and as part of the same effort, the trade unions and their members behaved in a manner which is not consistent with the view that full employment must always lead to rapid wage increases and that, at favourable times, trade union leaders must always be expected to press for everything that can be obtained for their members. The policy of wage restraint was most faithfully observed. In the two and a half years up to September, 1950, wage rates rose by only 5 per cent. This, again, is not necessarily to approve of wage stops of this kind—they are crude weapons which impede the proper distribution of labour and create inequities. But it can be said that in this period communal common sense was in charge in a manner which many, perhaps most, people, thinking of these problems before 1945, would have thought inconceivable.

These are, of course, but scraps of comfort, and it would be foolish to generalize upon them. But they do suggest that whole communities can exercise economic discretion. And if, as in Great Britain, they can behave in this fashion at unlikely times—for it must not be overlooked that this was a period when the Socialists were in power for the first time and the wage earners would be forgiven for a feeling of heady success in the existence of what they thought was a government of their own—must we assume that nothing better can be done when more is known of the dangers, as well as the merits, of a full employment policy, and when the appropriate institutional checks and safeguards have been erected against these dangers ?

But the pity of it all is that Eucken is no longer with us to help to answer such questions. They seem to me matters which cannot be resolved either by abstract reasoning or by the study of past events taken separately. They call for theoretical analysis against the background of the institutional forms of our day. It was precisely that approach which Eucken did so much to foster in Germany in arguments which fortunately are now available for English readers, in his recently published *The Foundations of Economics*. In that larger book he makes the plea for a more balanced and synthesized approach to economic events. In this present shorter essay he gives us a sample of the illumination which can be spread by adopting it.

JOHN JEWKES.

I

IDEAS AND EXPERIMENTS

THE world has been in a state of upheaval since the end
of the eighteenth century, when the Industrial Revolution began in this country and from there spread out
vigorously on all sides. The European and American
continents were the first to be affected. Expanding
continuously, this secular movement to-day also affects
Russia, East Asia and all other countries where there is
any possibility of industrial and technical development.
In the older industrial countries, however, industrialization has already passed through many greatly varied
stages during the last one hundred and fifty years.

How can modern industrialized economy and society
be organized in a humane and efficient way? That
is the problem with which every nation is confronted.
That it is a specifically modern problem we recognize
the more clearly, the further industrialization pro-
gresses ; yet the economic doctrines that now prevail
over most of humanity and determine economic policy,
were developed a long time ago. They are a com-
pound of the Mercantilist ideas of the eighteenth
century, of the Liberal ideas of the eighteenth and
nineteenth century, and of Socialist ideas that mainly
arose during the first half of the nineteenth century ;
but those mid-century Liberals, or Sismondi, or the
Saint-Simonists, or Marx—in short all the thinkers of
that time—lived in an economic society quite different
from ours. In it, the problem of labour for industry
was already beginning to make itself felt, but it was
not at all the same as it is to-day. All that was known
was the pre-industrial economy and the beginning of
the great change. "Trusts," cartels, trade unions,
central banks, either did not exist or were only just

beginning to develop. There had been no experience of centralized control of industry. Yet this bygone age evolved doctrines which prevail to-day, and formulated conceptions that most people still use—e.g. " Socialism " and " Capitalism." But the rapid advance of technical progress, industrialization, mass concentration and urbanization, has changed the content of all economic problems. Yesterday's ideas are old and outmoded. There exists a discrepancy between realities and ideologies which is of vital importance to economic action.

In a situation of this kind it is imperative that past ideologies should be set aside and full value given to experience. The last half-century in particular has taught us much with its rapid changes of economic policy, its interventionism, full employment policies, and the experiments in centralization carried out by Russia, Germany and other countries. After 1914, experiments were made with new forms of currency, with market control, economic self-government, corporations, central planning, etc., without anyone knowing what the outcome would be. Now things are different. The knowledge gained from such experiments is available. We are now in a position to learn from the recent past and to make use of it for the future. A new style of economic policy is possible—and essential —if we are to extricate ourselves from this unsuccessful age. What we must do is to turn away from ideology and accept the lessons of experience ; for we still have no answer to the problem of how to organize an industrialized economy humanely and efficiently.

In 1827 Sismondi wrote : " The existence of society is now determined by quite new factors, of which we still have no experience whatsoever." But now, one hundred and twenty years later, we have very wide economic and social experience, and it is the essential task of scholarship to assess this experience and make it useful for the future.

To assist in this task is also the purpose of this short book in which I shall attempt a brief assessment of German economic experience since the beginning of the century. Germany has lived through a great deal during the last fifty years and has made many economic experiments. From her experience may, I think, be derived certain economic principles of general application. From German economic policy of the recent past we can learn lessons which will be of assistance in framing future economic and social policy in general.

Economic policy at the beginning of the century is habitually referred to as " *laissez-faire*." What exactly was this ? It is usually said to have been a period of economic freedom from state influence ; but a glance at the realities of the situation, as obtaining in Germany, for instance, shows that to call it that is quite wrong. The beginning of this century was, in fact, a period when the state introduced legislation strictly defining and limiting the rights of property, contract and association, as well as laws governing patents and copyright. At that time Germany, like other states, possessed a constitution designed to create an efficient machinery of state and to protect the freedom of the individual. She, in common with other states, possessed a legal code, and the scope of general civil law, commercial law, etc., was very wide. The daily workings of every firm and household proceeded within the framework of legal norms laid down by the state, whether it was a question of buying or selling, being granted credit or engaging a workman. But the economic system and the shaping of it were not regarded as a special responsibility of the state.

The conviction prevailing in Germany and elsewhere at that time was that, within the limits of the law, social forces would spontaneously generate a good economic system. Such was the economic policy of *laissez-faire*. There was also freedom to determine the forms of the everyday economic process. Markets in which com-

petition prevailed could, for instance, be transformed
into markets with a seller's monopoly. The economic
system is the sum total of forms assumed by the daily
workings of the economic process ; and, though the
state at that time did attempt to regulate the economic
system in certain respects—as in the case of banks of
issue and international trade treaties, the system was
on the whole left in the hands of private enterprise.
The gist of the matter is that in those days industrial
enterprises could not only initiate their everyday
economic processes, buying and selling freely and at
prices not fixed by the state, but they could also modify
the system—for instance, by forming a cartel. Both the
economic process and the economic system were at
that time mainly left to private enterprise.

Economic policy entered upon a new phase after the
1914–18 war. Then began the period of experiment in
which we still are. To a greater or lesser degree both
the economic process and the economic system became
determined, regulated or influenced by the state. A
new type of economic politician emerged everywhere :
the experimenter. Rathenau and Schacht are German
representatives of the type.

Experiment began in Germany with the 1919
Socialization Laws. A somewhat calmer period followed these, but then came the great Crisis of 1929–32
which instigated further experimentation on novel
lines. A policy of full employment, tried out on a large
scale after 1933, was combined with experiments in
assigning a leading economic role to certain corporations or classes. It is significant that this policy of full
employment was followed by one of central economic
control, particularly after 1936. The great experiment
with central control lasted until 1948 and was characterized by an attempt to exert decisive influence upon
even everyday economic processes by means of directives
from central planning offices—without, however, abolish-
ing private ownership of the means of production. A

further phase of experimentation began only recently with the 1948 Currency Reform.

However these experiments may have worked out in detail, they certainly have positive significance in one respect : they have considerably enriched our economic experience. And experience is just what we need. Let us benefit from it by observing how certain major problems were dealt with by German economic policy from 1900 to the present day and with what results.

First and foremost there is the problem of *economic power*.

The Reich Courts defined their attitude to the formation of cartels in a famous judgment given on 4th February 1897, by which cartel agreements were declared to be admissible and sanctions against outsiders were allowed. The Reich Courts took the view that those engaged in a branch of trade in which prices were sinking too low could combine, and that such combination was in the general interest. It was particularly significant that the Reich Courts went so far as to authorize drastic methods of direct economic warfare, such as the boycott, the principle of which was not to outstrip a competitor by superior achievement, but to damage him by interfering with and undermining his business relationships. Cartels and other forms of monopoly were thus granted the privilege of using offensive methods. On this legal basis cartels and related forms were able to develop in Germany. Statistics for 1905 recorded a total of 385. The industries most affected were : coal mining, iron and steel, potash mining, bricks and cement.

This attitude to the cartel problem was of fundamental importance, for it meant that the right of freedom of contract could also be used to eliminate competition and to restrict the freedom of others by means of sanctions, boycotts, etc. The principle of freedom of contract had thus come into open conflict with the competitive principle.

Legislation in the age of *laissez-faire* never really attempted any fundamental settlement of this conflict, which was continually flaring up and engaged the attention of the courts again and again. As Heckscher says : "Liberalism never wholly sided with free competition against freedom of contract, nor with the latter against the former." This was the case in Germany, too. Freedom of contract was actively exploited to bring about a state of affairs in which freedom of contract in effect ceased to exist. The principle of freedom of contract would, for instance, be invoked in support of the formation of a coal syndicate, as a result of which certain coal merchants and consumers were deprived of all freedom of contract, because they became dependent on a single supplier and had to accept his conditions.

In the Age of Experiment, the period after the first world war, the problem of economic power prompted novel and varied economic measures.

First in order of time came the experiment of the Socialization Laws of 1919. The underlying idea of these laws was to give a compulsory character to the existing coal and potash mining syndicates. Thus, freedom of enterprise was eliminated in the case of coal and potash, in as much as all enterprises were compelled to join the syndicates. The syndicates were to be "self-governing bodies," and they were to provide economic leadership and were to be managed not only by the owners, but also by representatives of the workers and consumers. The formation of such self-governing bodies was, therefore, also intended to solve the social problem. The old private power groups became compulsory corporations, thereby increasing their power, but they were in future to have a socialized character. The opposing interests of employers and employed, coal producers and coal consumers, were to be reconciled by the participation of all concerned in economic control. It was hoped, above all, that the problem of economic power could be solved by the co-operation of the workers' representatives. The inclusion of miners' and employees' delegates in the management of these self-governing coal mining bodies was designed to ensure consideration of the interests of the community as a whole. Differences were to be bridged at the conference table. The admission of all interested parties was to make the old power groups into " socialized " corporations.

The experiment failed ; and the reason why it failed illustrates an important principle : if the workers share in the profits of monopoly, they have as much interest in the monopoly as the owners. This was the case in Germany, where the mine-workers agreed to demands for an increase in coal prices whenever it meant a parallel increase in their wages. The participation of workers' delegates in the management of the monopolies merely broadened their base, and the result was that workers and owners combined in a single monopolistic group which had little consideration for the rest of the community. The law did not work out as Rathenau, for instance, had hoped ; and a subsidiary measure was introduced whereby increases in coal prices had to receive the consent of the state. This proved extremely effective. Otherwise, however, the power of monopoly was strengthened and by no means controlled by the workers' delegates.

Keynes and others thought that the ideal size of an organizational unit of industry lay somewhere between the individual and the modern state, and that the recognition of semi-autonomous bodies within the framework of the state represented a step forward. He and others believed that these bodies or groups could work for the common good. German experience has not confirmed that hope : it did not work out like that either in the coal mining or potash industries, nor in the later compulsory corporations of the National Socialist period, for corporations of this kind do not moderate individual self-interest. It is, in fact, the reverse that is true : " group egoism " tends to expand, because

C

groups have power.   Nor do such groups by any means
aim at serving the interests of the community.   Their
representatives struggle against other groups, and
against the state, in the real or supposed interests of
their own group.   In the language of the economist
there arises an antagonism of bilateral monopolies, in
which only an unstable state of equilibrium tending
towards disequilibrium is achieved.   " Group anarchy "
—inter-group conflict—is the result.   We have lived
through a great deal of that in Germany.

With the Cartel Act of November 1923 Germany
made a further innovatory approach to the problem of
economic power.   This Act, which excluded coal and
potash mining, represented a first attempt in Germany
to counteract *abuse* of economic power.   The principle
underlying this important Act was that cartel agreements were to be legalized.   So they remained recognized
by the law.   But they were made subject to state supervision.   To this end a special government department
and a Cartel Tribunal were set up.   Among other things,
the consent of the president of the Tribunal had to be
obtained whenever a cartel wished to force an outsider
to join by threatening sanctions and other measures.

This experiment was energetically carried out, and it,
too, achieved a surprising and unintended result.   At
first, the cartels and their supporters bitterly opposed
state supervision as an outrageous encroachment on
freedom of enterprise ; but that soon changed.   When
the Ministry of Economics began to counter cartel
abuses by encouraging competition and loosening up
markets, the bitterness of the cartels turned against the
institution of Free Competition.   They denounced it
as " reactionary Manchesterism " and, by contrast,
praised the cartel principle as a higher form of economic
development.   State supervision, on the other hand,
they viewed with less misgiving, especially as they had
been successful in arousing sympathy for the cartels,
even among the trade unions.   So the interested parties

ceased to oppose the popular institution of state control,
but persevered all the more strongly against the method
of encouraging competition.   There took place a flight
of industry away from competition into the realm of
state control and cartels.   The number of German
cartels increased remarkably, and in 1925 there were
2,500.

The results of the 1923 Cartel Act enable us to
establish the following principle :   monopoly control
directed against so-called " abuse " of economic power
is bound to fail.   The conception of " abuse " cannot
be defined exactly.   The point needs emphasizing that
once monopolistic bodies have begun to flourish in a
state, they gain considerable political influence, so
considerable that the state itself becomes incapable of
exercising effective control.   Economic policy, therefore,
should not direct itself against abuse of power by existing
monopolies, but rather against their very existence.
Otherwise it has no chance of settling the problem.

German economic policy, however, took a different
course.   It was widely held in Germany, and is still so
held in many other countries even to-day, that the
problem of economic power in private hands can only
be solved by the state transferring that power into its
own hands.

Germany made two experiments in this direction :
one in transferring the power to state central planning
offices while maintaining private ownership ;   the other
in nationalization ;   these being the two possibilities.

We shall have more to say later about how and why
Germany, after 1936, went over to a policy of increasing
economic control by central planning offices.   Here we
are concerned with the effects of that development.
As far as the syndicates were concerned, though they
remained in existence, their function was changed.
They became departments of the central administration.
The pig-iron syndicate, for example, henceforth made
central allocations of pig-iron that it had previously

sold monopolistically. The staff and internal organization of the syndicates remained essentially the same.
The iron and chemical industry " concerns " also fitted
easily into the structure of central economic administration. Erstwhile private power groups—syndicates
and " concerns "—were now reduced to the function of
receiving the general production directives issued by the
central planning offices, working them out with respect
to particular firms, forwarding them and supervising
their execution. Conversely, these power groups continued to exert considerable influence by inspiring the
central planning offices, the heads of which frequently
stood in close personal contact with them. War-time
Germany thus developed a somewhat peculiar economic
system. Whereas the economy was officially directed
by central planning offices, the planners' decisions were
in fact often strongly influenced by private bodies, e.g.
" concerns ' —as, for instance, in the allocation of raw
materials. What emerged, therefore, was a peculiar
fusion of private and central administrative powers.

This was an aggravation rather than a solution of the
problem of economic power. Small and medium
enterprises lost ground. Nor, as we shall see, was the
social problem solved by central controls, but rendered
more acute. All this served to demonstrate an economic
principle, the importance of which cannot be sufficiently
emphasized—namely, that *the problem of economic power
can never be solved by further concentrations of power.*

But what was Germany's experience of *nationalization*
in connection with monopolies and other power groups ?
Experiments of this nature first took the form of national-
izing electricity, gas, railways, etc., but are to-day
proceeding on a very much larger scale with the
nationalization of whole industries in the Eastern Zone.

Let us first consider what was achieved by the
nationalization of individual monopolies such as railways and electricity. State monopolies have regularly
adopted the same monopolistic policy as private mono-

polies. In just the same way they strive to reach the point of maximum net profit, which in the case of monopoly usually falls appreciably short of the point of optimum service. Indeed, the tendency to exploit monopolistic position to the utmost was often more evident in state than in private monopolies. A state monopoly feels justified in taking this course, because its profits benefit the state or the municipality, thereby constituting an indirect tax not used for private purposes.

Nationalization amalgamates economic and political power. Uniting the rival spheres of economy and state, it is a form of concentration that renews and increases the problem of power.

Developments in the Eastern Zone confirm what has been said, except that there the danger manifests itself quite differently and to a far greater degree. The economy is dominated by a stratum of officials administering the nationalized enterprises. This concentration of power increases dependence and still further restricts freedom. In many cases whole trades, e.g. the butchers', are wiped out, and instead the population is supplied with meat by a single state organization. Both the workers and the consumers become dependent on the central state administration controlling these organizations.

German experience therefore enables us to state precisely on what lines a solution of the problem of economic power should *not* be attempted. The solution is not a policy of *laissez-faire* which permits misuses of freedom of contract to destroy freedom : nor is it a system of monopoly control which permits the formation of monopolies while merely seeking to check abuses. Over and above this, it has been shown that the problem of economic power cannot be solved by further concentrations of power, whether in the form of a corporative system—as in German coal mining—or of centralized economic control, or of nationalization. Power remains power whoever may exercise it, and it is in public rather than private hands that power reaches its zenith.

Let us return to consideration of the problem itself. Is the problem of economic power really so urgent? Why do we give it priority? The answer is that power constantly confronts men and politics with a dilemma. History is full of abuse of power. The possession of power provokes arbitrary action, endangers the freedom of other people, and destroys mature and good institutions. Nevertheless, without positions of power there can be no social life; for there *must* be authority—in the state and in a firm.

Adherents of power minimize its dangers, and opponents its indispensability. The immense practical problem is thus obscured. Even the great historian, Jacob Burckhardt, confused the essential issue. For him, power was an evil in itself; but, at the same time, he regarded the state as a benefactor. Yet no state can exist without power. The discovery of a way out of this dilemma is perhaps the most vital task of all politics, including economic politics.

The problem of economic power has always existed, but since the Industrial Revolution it has been posed in a new form. That revolution initiated an age of proliferating economic power, and, ever since, the economic development of industrial countries has been marked by the existence of excessive economic power. In Germany, and other industrial countries, there have been examples of such excessive power being wielded by individual firms, " concerns," cartels, central planning agencies, or even by trade unions.

A few comments on German experience may serve to illustrate the effects of private economic power; but first there is one point to be made.

Monopolistic enterprises often invest relatively heavily, and rapidly renew their productive apparatus in order to bring it into line with the latest technical knowledge. Observation of this fact has led some writers—e.g. Schumpeter—to consider a seller's monopoly particularly efficient. A monopolistic firm producing shoe-making machines can devote its monopoly profits to investment and to permanent improvement of its plant. Thanks to a monopoly position and in terms of monopolistically increased shoe prices, this firm can extract sums for investment from shoe factories and ultimately from purchasers of shoes. " Forced saving " is not only brought about by modern machinery of credit, but also by monopolies. The purchaser of shoes, the consumer, is forced to restrict his consumption, that is, to deny himself, to some extent, the use of means of production, e.g. those producing textile goods, houses, and so on. The flow of capital is therefore preferentially diverted from other branches of production to the manufacture of shoe-making machines ; whereas the economic point of view demands that the shortage of all goods should be overcome in right proportion. It is true that monopoly enables this firm both to attract more capital to itself and to make the excess investment profitable. Without monopoly, the firm would have invested less and renewed its plant less rapidly ; but other branches of production would have had more means at their disposal and—most important of all— the supply of consumer goods in general would have been better. Economically speaking, there is therefore no sense in admiring the technical apparatus of monopolists. So much by way of briefly exemplifying the economic effects of monopoly.

It has, however, its effects on other aspects of human affairs. A cardinal principle of the constitutional state is that individual rights and liberties should be safeguarded against violation by fellow-citizens on the one hand and by the state on the other—above all, against the compulsory power of state administrative organs. Private economic powers are, however, in a position to deprive others of their constitutional liberties. Around 1910, for instance, for a German firm wishing to deal in cement the right to trade freely remained purely nominal, if the cement syndicate applied sanctions and

refused all supplies.   Similarly, freedom to combine
became compulsion when private industrial cartels
forced individual firms to join by threatening sanctions.
But as soon as the economy became controlled by
central planning offices instead of by private bodies,
as after 1936, the threat to individual rights and
liberties came from the opposite quarter.   The cement
merchant in question became dependent on the decisions of the cement planning office.   Whether the
firm was accepted as a distributor of cement and how
much cement it received, was decided by the public
planning office.   Even though solemnly guaranteed by
the constitution, freedom in the choice and pursuit of
trade became abolished by economic policy, in that
state administrative action overrode it.   The private
threat to freedom disappeared ; but the other threat,
from the state itself, increased considerably.   In the
first case, the safeguard against arbitrary action by
private enterprise proved of no avail against the power
of private syndicates.   In the second case, it failed to
prevent organs of state from infringing private rights,
because the central planning offices had to be given
power to carry out their task.

It could be shown how private power groups and
central planning offices also changed the political life
and the structure of the German state.   The problem of
economic power *is the obverse aspect of the problem of
freedom* in a modern industrialized economy.   Various
attempts to solve it have been made in Germany, and
they have failed.

II

INEVITABILITY OF DEVELOPMENT

THE study of economic and social power, and of all other problems of political economy, is influenced by the widely held view that modern technology inevitably leads to large-scale mechanization and organization and therewith to concentration and monopoly, and finally to central control. It is believed, in short, that modern technology kills competition.

This, too, is an early nineteenth-century view. Yet even to-day it is still a starting point for most reflections on the economic future. Marx supported it by accumulating evidence from the early industrial history of England, and gave it driving force by discovering and effectively formulating a law of concentration which, as he believed, determined historical development. According to Marx, the very large spinning mill must oust the small, the medium and ultimately the large spinning mills. The present level of technical achievement or—as Marx formulated it—" the stage reached in the development of material forces of production " must necessitate the concentration of production in one or a few large-scale works and must inevitably lead to monopoly.

Views of this type have been reiterated ever since, though admittedly without complete agreement. Some believe perfect competition to be as lacking in equilibrium as it is unrealizable—thus Marx, and, latterly, Schumpeter. Others think it would lead to general equilibrium, but can no longer be realized to-day. The former think that perfect competition is bad and dead, and the latter that it is good but dead. The difference between them need not concern us here. Both agree that modern technology concentrates production and economic power, and that competition is doomed to vanish from modern economy.

If this fundamental assumption is correct, no policy directed against the building up of economic power is wise or stands a chance. Instead, economic and, above all, social policy will have to conform to the inevitable development of monopoly and central planning.

Whether this hypothesis is correct, is what we must find out. Is it confirmed by economic developments in Germany ?

Experience gives a strange answer to this question. In *one* respect it partially confirms the old hypothesis ; for if monopoly is already far advanced in an industry, then there is in fact a tendency towards central control, central planning and, eventually, nationalization. But this only applies to major industries—for example, German coal mining. The seller's monopoly of major industries or bilateral monopolies with markets in disequilibrium, as it were, provokes central planning. The step forward to central planning is not necessary, though it is not infrequently taken. There remains, however, the question—and this is the other and crucial aspect of the matter—whether monopoly and the decline of competition really are inevitable developments. What are the facts ?

Contrary to the prevailing hypothesis, what modern technology released in Germany was in fact an extremely marked tendency towards competition that increased from decade to decade and became far more powerful in the twentieth century than in the nineteenth, although increasingly radical steps were taken against it.

Modern technology increased competition—in the strict sense of the word—in three ways :

Firstly, the remarkable improvement and cheapening of transport caused many local markets to merge and lose their independence. Sellers previously enjoying local oligopoly or monopoly, entered into competition with one another. This can be illustrated from the history of practically every agricultural or industrial enterprise. Late in the nineteenth century, for instance, a certain engineering factory was still almost exclusively supplying joiners in a local market, which it more or less monopolized. But with the expansion of rail, water and road transport, this firm widened its market area and at the same time found outsiders competing in its original sphere of monopoly. It has often been described how, from the eighteen-seventies onwards, falling rail and sea transport costs stimulated competition on the European grain markets ; and this is merely a cross section of a universal phenomenon. The rapid development of communications—telegraph, telephone and wireless—contributed no less effectively to the merging of market areas. Local raw material and grain markets vanished and with them went many opportunities to form monopolies and oligopolies. Furthermore, improved techniques of communication perfected the machinery of competition on many markets for raw materials, semi-manufactured goods and even for finished goods.

The revolutionary effects of this development on labour markets invite special attention. The mid-nineteenth-century industrial worker's choice was still restricted to the one or two firms with places of work near his home. The employer often enjoyed a buyer's monopoly or oligopoly of his labour market. The situation changed with the expansion of railways and the coming of motor transport and bicycles. Many workers now travel considerable distances to their work ; and as a result the areas drawn on for labour by individual firms have expanded and merged. In Germany the radius of such an area may be as much as 45 to 50 miles. This has completely changed the form of labour markets. Workers now have a far wider choice of employer. Hitherto dormant competition has been brought to life—by modern technology.

Secondly, competition was unexpectedly stimulated
by technical progress in the development of substitutes.
This fundamental factor was beyond the ken of the
early nineteenth-century thinkers, but their modern
successors should take it into account. The development of artificial silk, cellulose wool, nylon and other
fibres ; the emergence of oil as a rival to coal ; new
building materials competing with bricks ; porcelain
substitutes and synthetic rubber—all these are but
a few examples of the universally increasing competition
of substitutes. The resulting elasticity of demand for
individual commodities brings the market nearer to
perfect competition, even if the seller of any particular
type of commodity is a monopolist, since monopolies
are forced to behave as though they were in competition.
Brickwork cartels, for example, have to reckon with
the rivalry of the new building materials, that is, with
a greater elasticity of demand ; similarly railways in
face of the increasing competition of motor transport.
Substitute-competition has become so general that it
now affects the buying and selling decisions of every
firm and household.

Thirdly, and lastly : recent advances of technical
knowledge have greatly enhanced the flexibility of the
modern industrial apparatus. There has been a marked
increase in the ability of factories engaged in the later
stages of the manufacturing process to change their
market by switching rapidly from one type of manufacture to another. This development became very
evident during the two world wars, taking even experts by surprise and vitally influencing the course of
events. Watch factories were very rapidly converted
to the manufacture of fuses, and engineering factories
to shells and U-boat parts. Within a short space of
time a major part of industrial production had been
converted in this way. The reverse process took place
after the wars when factories were, for instance, recon-
verted from guns to machines or from tanks to lorries.

Flexibility is, however, no less effective in peace than in war. Flexibility of production is a conception capable of being narrowly defined as the ability of a firm to switch its production rapidly from one market to another, and during the last half century it has increased in Germany to an unusual degree.

In contrast to conditions still obtaining at the beginning of the century, there is now constant variation in the production programme of firms engaged in later stages of manufacture. For example, a factory producing stoves also takes up the manufacture of refrigerators and later of radio sets, and thus competes in new markets. Another firm, offering a special type of pump in an oligopolistic market, abandons the struggle and produces agricultural machinery instead. A third firm switches from pedal bicycles to motor bicycles ; a fourth firm, now producing optical instruments, began by manufacturing locks. Production programmes and the articles produced are changed from year to year—according to the opportunities for profit. Firms in these industries are constantly deciding what they will produce next and their choice is by no means predetermined. If switching were not hampered by patents and licences, the transfer of firms from market to market would be even more pronounced, corresponding to the capacities of modern technology, particularly modern engineering techniques. Sellers on most markets for manufactures must, therefore, reckon constantly with the appearance of new and efficient competitors.

The situation is different in the raw material industries, for example coal, pig-iron or electric power. These do in fact produce essentially the same thing year after year, and a change of production programme is technically difficult or only possible within narrow limits. *Direct* flexibility is therefore slight or absent in works of this kind. Nevertheless, there is a considerable measure of *indirect* flexibility. Coal, electric power and pig-iron can serve an almost unlimited number of purposes. This makes it possible for the goods they are instrumental in producing to vary constantly and to enter into competition with different goods. Electric power is used by a firm which first manufactures drugs and then goes over to the production of other chemical goods, thereby bringing electric power products into competition on new markets. Modern technical developments have further reinforced competition by very greatly widening the range of uses to which raw materials can be put. Coal, for example, is no longer solely a fuel but also the raw material of dyes, medicines, nitrogen fertilizers, etc., so that coal products appear on the most widely varied markets. Flexibility of production and increased competition here make themselves indirectly felt while directly affecting industries engaged in later stages of manufacture.

This fact is, however, veiled by certain ideas which create illusory economic problems. The centenarian view still prevails that modern techniques of production deprive undertakings of flexibility in response to changing market needs. It is thought that capital is largely tied up, no longer withdrawable, and bound to particular technical methods of production, so that losses cannot be circumvented and production cannot be switched to more promising markets. Modern production is imagined to be rigid, adjusted only to the manufacture of certain commodities, technically incapable of flexibility. This rigidity of supply is set in opposition to the rapidly varying nature of demand, and from the antithesis is constructed a huge economic problem. But this view contradicts all the realities of the situation. It is true that around 1850 or 1900 technical immaturity gave industrial production a certain rigidity, long since outgrown. It is true that even to-day capital invested in, say, a chemical factory cannot be withdrawn in order to build a water works instead. But that chemical factory can rapidly change the markets for which it caters. In the chemical industry, as in engineering, shoe-making, etc., production plans are constantly being readjusted to the profitability of various markets, even where much capital is tied up in plant.

" Fixed costs " do not mean " fixed production." Directly or indirectly, technical progress has imparted a high degree of flexibility to modern production. Anyone inspecting the day-to-day programme of work done in a steel rolling mill will see just how much flexible adjustment to differing orders goes on—despite high fixed costs.

Widening markets, growing use of substitutes and increasing flexibility of production, these are all factors which reinforce the element of competition.

This, however, is only one side of the question. We have on the one hand this marked competitive tendency unleashed by modern technology which is taking increasing effect the more it develops ; on the other, we have the reaction to it. Successful attempts have been, and are being, made to contain or repel the general advance of competition. Economic policy in Germany, for instance, can hardly be said to have proceeded on the assumption that competition was declining. On the contrary, the struggle against competition has engrossed a major part of German economic policy. The universal tendency towards monopoly became the more effective, the more individual enterprises lost their old monopolistic or oligopolistic positions and were drawn into competition. State economic policy also worked against competition—mostly under pressure from interested parties. Since the eighteen-seventies, tariffs, import prohibitions, control of foreign exchange holdings and other measures of economic policy have been adopted in turn to combat the competition arising from cheapening transport facilities. The elimination of increasing " substitute-competition " proved more difficult. An example is the development of motor transport—an achievement, that is, of modern technology—which confronted the Reich Railways and its monopolistic positions with numerous efficient competitors. By the Emergency Decree of October 1931 this new competition was largely eliminated, and a compulsory state cartel was set up to prevent competitors from making full use of their competitive powers. Finally there are the various methods used to suppress competition arising from the increasing elasticity of industrial production, for example : patents, patent associations, state prohibitions of investment, bans on admission, and other restrictions of the right to trade freely. All this constitutes a vast system of private and state measures designed to weaken or destroy the tendency towards perfect competition in modern economy. No one investigating any modern industrial undertaking can fail to be impressed by this state of affairs. *The tension between increasing competition and the forces counter-acting it is a fundamental factor in recent German economic history.*

According to the old school of thought, still represented to-day by Schumpeter, for example, modern technology demands huge industrial units, destroys small and medium works, and gives rise to inherent conflicts between the size of works, the rigidity of supply and the varying nature of demand to which production is no longer able to adapt itself. Competition is therefore regarded as an antiquated system, perhaps of some use previously, but obsolete now that the economy is regulated by the emergence of " concerns," trusts, cartels and other monopolies, state intervention, corporations, full employment policies and central planning. This is the usual picture of modern economic development, but it needs to be reversed if it is to correspond to realities—at any rate in Germany. Far from being the product of an inevitable process of development, modern economic policy is a defensive reaction against a definite historical tendency towards competition. This is the only possible interpretation of German economic policy in recent decades.

Let us develop this argument in terms of a single illustrative case, by describing the process of economic concentration.

The impression exists in many quarters that technology causes production to be concentrated in a very few huge, monopolistic works that have destroyed all smaller competitors. In practice it is true that there has been a considerable growth in the size of blast furnaces, rolling mills, engineering factories and other industrial works, and that this growth has in fact been stimulated by technical developments. But this is not industrial concentration. The economic power of any single blast furnace or spinning mill, however large, does not in itself amount to much. The expansion of markets has been proportionately much greater, and such big works usually contribute only a modicum of the total supplies. The same thing holds true of a shoe factory or an automobile works.

The true characteristic of concentration is rather *the bringing of many works under unified control*, as when several artificial silk factories are subordinated to the direction of a single " concern," or when a number of collieries, blast furnaces, rolling mills, engineering works, etc., are concentrated vertically under a single controlling organization. I. G. Farben or United States Steel own, or owned, hundreds of works. Even small or medium-sized undertakings often own several small works, for instance a medium-sized engineering factory owning a foundry and a plug factory. The same applies on a large scale to " concerns." Furthermore, cartel formation associates several firms, each often owning several works. Thus an individual colliery is only one of many belonging to the firm K., which in turn is only one of many members of the coal syndicate. A medium pharmaceutical works employing two hundred workers in the town of G. belongs to a

D

" concern " that owns, amongst other things, ten other chemical factories and is a member of various cartels. This is the way in which concentration works out in practice, whereas what Marx envisaged was a whole market supplied by a single giant pharmaceutical works.

The decisive factor is not the expansion of individual works resulting from developments in technology, but the control of many works by few firms, or by a single firm.

Of course there are exceptions which, however, should not be over estimated. In certain branches of production, the size of works is such that, given an optimum plant, the output of a single works is sufficient for the optimum supply of a market, so that several works of the same kind would not be able to sell at prices covering their costs. Municipal tramways or spiral spring or bottle-making factories are examples of cases where technical development makes it most efficient for a single works to dominate the market. As a rule, however, industrial concentration consists in several works being brought under unified control.

Where this has been done, it has been for several reasons of a legal and political, rather than of a technical, nature. The following are just some of these.

(1) The introduction of customs tariffs greatly increased the ability of protected German industries to form cartels, by making it possible for them to isolate and monopolize the German market. The incentive to form a monopoly is strongest where a branch of industry is able to supply the home market single-handedly, but can only take full advantage of tariff protection by forming a cartel. Numerous examples are to be found in the history of the German iron industry.

(2) Concentration has been greatly fostered by patent laws. Not only have patents given a monopoly position to individual firms, but, what is more im-

portant, they have broken up or consolidated the formation of cartels or " concerns." Apart from actual patent cartels or patent trusts, the exchange of licences has facilitated cartel formation generally, many cartels being kept together by the fact that breakaway members would lose the right to certain patents. Moreover patents have had a decisive influence in the formation of " concerns " whose object is to exercise patent rights and resist outsiders. In general, patents and trade marks, and the accompanying price-fixing and advertisement, making use of techniques of suggestion, have virtually contributed to the prevalence of monopoly or oligopoly in modern German economy, as elsewhere : for example, the building up of " concerns " in the chemical, washing-powder and cigarette industries.

(3) One of the characteristics of an experimental economic policy is its extreme instability. It is subject to continual changes in currency, trade, fiscal and wage policies, etc., which have in their turn considerably increased the element of uncertainty in the planning of individual firms. Risks are appreciably greater. The gap between planned and actual dates has widened. Due to this instability of economic policy, firms have to reckon with the fact that their whole basis of calculation may be changed within a short space of time. This vitally affects the volume of investment.

This instability of economic policy is also another factor that has greatly encouraged economic concentration. The greater the risk, the greater the incentive to form " concerns," especially the type of " concern " embracing different industries or different parts of the same industry or trade. The uncertainty aroused by rapid changes of economic policy prompts firms to participate in or to buy up firms in other branches of production ; thus we find a cotton mill, for instance, interested in a coal merchants, an engineering factory and a candle factory. This is one of the many ways in which economic policy has itself fostered industrial concentration.

There is an objection to explaining concentration as I have done, namely that larger works applying new techniques often destroy or threaten small firms using older methods. It is pointed out that many craftsmen —in textiles and milling, for example—have been forced out of business, and that the existence of many small lime kilns or old-fashioned acetic acid works is threatened by modern large-scale works with lower production costs. Is this not, it is asked, a factor making for concentration ?

The answer is that such cases have been and still are frequent. They give rise to grave social problems, in particular the question of how production can rapidly reassimilate the employees of these obsolete works. Moreover, partial concentration really does take place, in that production is carried on by one works instead of by dozens or hundreds of firms, each with works of its own. Modern technology does in fact foster concentration—up to a point. Nevertheless, this new type of large-scale works—such as a weaving mill that ruins hundreds of small weavers in the same district—usually enters into competition with other new mills in a wider market. The history of many an industry in the nineteenth and twentieth centuries shows that the decline of small and medium firms, following the establishment of large-scale plants, does not mean the elimination of competition, which regains ground with the widening of markets and the development of substitutes. Furthermore, it is well known that new techniques—such as the small electric motor—have tended to reverse the process in a great many branches of industry as the effect of their use on costs has been in favour of the small and medium-sized works.

If the true relationship between technology, competition and monopoly is as I have briefly described it here, then the general problem is quite different from what the old view supposes it to be. I began by mentioning the assumption on which this old view is based, namely, that competition is doomed and therefore does not come into question as a possible system. This assumption is unfounded. Economic policy has not been driven by modern technology into a corner where it must adopt systems—such as central planning or compulsory corporations. What is obsolete is not so much competition itself, as the belief that competition is obsolete.

The development of modern technical knowledge has taken twofold effect : on the one hand it has led to the elimination of many small enterprises, while on the other it has fostered competition by inventing substitutes, widening markets and enhancing flexibility of production. The influence of technology on concentration has therefore been ambivalent. But whereas the process of elimination may have been to the fore in the earlier period of industrialization, the later period, above all since the beginning of the twentieth century, has witnessed a remarkable strengthening of competition brought about by technical progress. This is a fact of great importance. It is possible for economic policy to regulate the economy by harnessing the forces, in particular of modern technology, that make for competition.

The problem of economic power, as I have shown, is one of cardinal importance. The attempts of German economic policy to solve it have all failed. Other countries will have had similar experiences. The problem of power is not to be solved either by a policy of *laissez-faire* or by monopoly control, corporations, nationalization or central controls.

When economic policy has failed, it has often seemed to prove the hypothesis of an inevitable historical evolution of monopoly and controls. The iron law of evolution appeared to be able to override economic policy. But we have seen that this is not so. There is, on the contrary, a marked historical tendency towards increased competition, which has been opposed by economic policy. Even where it was recognized that there were harmful aspects to monopolies, these continued to be fostered indirectly though at the same time special cartel and monopoly legislation was attempted to remedy certain abuses. There are so many cases of the state taking direct action against monopoly powers, while indirectly doing much to promote their establishment, preservation and expansion, that the state's behaviour can best be likened to a heavy smoker who takes medicine to allay symptoms of nicotine poisoning, but goes on smoking as before. None is surprised that the smoker's health does not improve, any more than it was not surprising that the prevailing economic and legal policy permitted the continued expansion of monopolistic power, and that such preventive measures as were taken proved inadequate—as has been demonstrated in Germany, the United States and other industrial countries.

The problem of economic power can only be solved by an intelligent co-ordination of all economic and legal policy. Laws relating to joint stock companies should, for instance, avoid anything that encourages the growth of undertakings to proportions beyond what is compatible with technical efficiency ; and patent legislation, all too often used in support of monopolies, should once again be made to serve only its true purpose. Speaking more generally, any single measure of economic policy should, if it is to be successful, be regarded as part of a policy designed to establish and maintain *economic order as a whole*. For instance, it was clear from the start that nothing would be gained by breaking up the German cartels in 1947, if the economy was to be regulated by central planning offices instead. So, the breaking up of the cartels was not intelligently adapted to the existing structure as a whole. The same applies to legislation with regard to works committees, foreign exchange markets, business taxes, etc. No measures of that kind can have any real meaning, unless they are conceived within the framework of a comprehensive policy designed to establish and maintain some general system. The general line of economic policy should be considered *before* any individual measure. That is the conclusion I wish to emphasize as an important matter of principle.

III

THE SOCIAL PROBLEM, SOCIAL POLICY AND FULL EMPLOYMENT

Social security and social justice are the great questions of the hour. Since the beginning of industrialization, the social problem has become more and more the focal problem of human existence and a moving force in the history of our time. Its solution has had a prior claim on thought and action.

In Germany, as elsewhere, nineteenth-century Liberal legislation established the free labour contract, freedom of movement and private property rights. But whereas liberty and equality of rights were politically and legally safeguarded, the industrial workers were often not free economically or socially. They felt themselves at the mercy of the superior force of Capital. This superiority made itself felt in the labour market and in the individual firm. Bad living conditions, inadequate wages, long hours of work, impairment of health, were wrongs asking to be put right. Society began to split into antagonistic halves. The social question was even then more than a crisis in a particular sphere of life, and it has since become a problem concerning the whole of society.

The answer to the social problem of that time was a " social policy " of a particular kind which we might describe as " *ad hoc.*" In general this was typical of economic policy around 1900. Just as an agrarian policy was applied to agrarian problems and an artisan policy to artisan problems, so a social policy was devised for the social problem. That was a time when little attention was paid to the inter-connection of all sectors of economic policy, and each sector had its own *ad hoc* policy. German social policy consisted of state protective measures such as the prohibition of child labour, the statutory limitation of working hours, factory inspection, and insurance against sickness, accidents and disablement. As is well known, German social policy made considerable and rapid strides along these lines.

Successes were undoubtedly achieved, but the remarkable rise in the working class standard of living that took place during the nineteenth century and early in the twentieth is not attributable in the first place to this social policy, but was mainly the result of general economic and technical progress. The better the workers were equipped with machines and the greater the output per head, the higher wages could rise. Simultaneously another factor—one already known to us—made itself felt to an increasing extent. As a result of improved transport facilities, the areas drawn on for labour by industrial firms merged more and more, and the workers benefited increasingly from the competition of these firms for manpower. To this must be added the results of the workers' own endeavours, for the foundation and growth of trade unions gradually established a partial seller's monopoly in many sections of the labour market, which thus altered to the advantage of the workers.

The nature of the social problem changed in the age of experiment after the first world war. Previously it had been above all one of *inequality of distribution* that had prompted the social legislator to intervene ; but then a new problem came to the fore, that of *insecurity* in the special form of prolonged mass unemployment. We must not forget that this form of unemployment did not exist before 1914. But subsequently it became the dominating factor in social and economic policy, and indeed in all politics, those of Germany as well. It will be unnecessary to recall the mass unemployment of the world economic crisis. The yearly average of unemployed in Germany with a population of some 70 million was 1.9 million in 1929, over 3 million in

1930, 4½ million in 1931, 5½ million in 1932, and 4.8 million in 1933.

A new social policy developed in the face of this altered, or second, type of social problem. It was no longer enough to devise a few social measures in the old *ad hoc* style, and the social point of view now affected the entire body politic of German economy. Business policy and the shaping of the economic system became subordinated to the end of solving the new social problem. Two lines of development were of outstanding importance because of the principle involved : firstly, the formation of great social power groups, and, secondly, the policy of full employment.

After the first world war the trade unions and employers' associations built themselves up under the aegis of the state into two great opposing groups representing individual industries throughout Germany : for example, the unions and associations of the metallurgical, textile and paper industries. Henceforth wages were settled by central state-sponsored bargaining between the two groups. Although these organizations included by no means all workers and employers, they enjoyed a partial monopoly.

The mid-twenties, however, revealed the instability of labour markets dominated by opposed partial monopolists. The danger of strikes and lock-outs caused the state to intervene and appoint " conciliators " or state mediators. Negotiated wages and conditions of work were then often declared by the state to be binding or statutory throughout the industry. Here, we have further confirmation of the conclusion reached in the first chapter, that lack of stability leads progressively to state control. The conciliators very soon became more than mere mediators. Seeing no other hope of reaching agreement, they fixed wages themselves. In this way decisions about wage levels and conditions of work devolved more and more upon state organs, thereby developing a powerful tendency towards central control. The dissolution of both trade unions and employers' associations by the National Socialists after 1933 was merely the radical continuation of a tendency that had already been very marked. A corporative economy prepares the ground for central control.

The second development, that of the policy of full employment, originated in the great crisis of 1929. Characteristic symptoms of the situation at that time were : idle machinery ; accumulated stocks of raw materials, semi-manufactures and finished goods ; masses of unemployed, and non-liquid banks. The unemployed had to be given relief, and as unemployment increased, it cast fresh burdens on the budget, necessitating new taxes that further deepened the depression. Economic policy got into a vicious circle and unemployment rose cumulatively. In considering the historical course of those fateful years, it is worth noting that the idea of full employment was advocated in the German Ministry of Economics as early as 1931. Dr. Lautenbach, deservedly known as the German Keynes, was working there at that time, and it was he who drew up the plans for overcoming deflation. If the government then in power had accepted his proposals, there might perhaps never have been a National Socialist revolution. The most likely reason why the government did not do so, was because it was afraid of inflation, which had caused such devastation in Germany ten years previously. Be that as it may, after the 1933 revolution the plans were immediately taken up by the new government and a vigorous policy of full employment was pursued. To put it briefly, this policy consisted in the giving of state contracts—road-building contracts, for instance—and in the acceptance by the state of bills discounted by the Central Bank. For example, an iron merchant was indebted to the bank to the extent of 100,000 marks and owned a large stock of iron girders. Under the new policy a builder was allotted a big state contract and received state-accepted bills in payment. He discounted these bills—for, say, 100,000 marks—at the bank and, with the amount placed to his credit, paid the iron merchant, whose girders he had bought. What happened ? The bank's liquidity was restored ; for the iron merchant's debit account of 100,000 marks vanished and the bank received instead a bill for 100,000 marks eligible for discount at the Reichsbank and hence immediately convertible into cash. Simultaneously the iron merchant's stock was reduced, and new building took place, giving employment to previously unemployed workers. The upshot was a fall in unemployment and stocks, and improved liquidity for the banks. In 1937 unemployment fell below one million and then vanished completely.

But from 1936 on, prices began to rise. The number of bank debtors was scaled down ; so newly created money could no longer vanish so quickly into bank debtors accounts. Stocks of raw materials and semi-manufactures had also diminished. The rise in prices was checked in 1936 by a price-freeze, all prices being fixed at the level existing in September of that year. Consequently the prices in many markets were no longer equilibrium prices. For example, more iron and cement was demanded than could be supplied at the fixed price. So the next step was rationing and, therefore, centrally planned allocation of raw materials, for it could not be left to chance to decide which firms received pig-iron or cement or other important raw materials. The authorities intervened and allocated these raw materials according to priorities determined by themselves. The economy began to be steered by state central planning instead of by the price system as previously. Thus the policy of full employment, like the corporative structure of the labour market, resulted in a marked tendency towards central control of the economy. The one, like the other, was conducive to an unstable economic system with a tendency to move in the direction of central control. So there were two strong historical forces impelling German economic policy along the path to central control : firstly, the formation of comprehensive economic and social pressure groups, and secondly, the policy of full employment.

This brings us to the great question : What were the social effects of the planned economy which was established in Germany in 1936 and which lasted until 1948 ? This question has to be asked and answered if the policy of full employment is to be given its due. Otherwise the argument about it remains incomplete.

Marx and his successors are notoriously of the opinion that central controls and collectivization can solve the social problem. According to Marx, private ownership of the means of production is the primary cause of the social problem. In his view, capitalist private property, based on the exploitation of outside and only nominally free labour, leads to a monopoly of capital by a few capitalists and to the complete dependence of the proletariat. Capitalist production thus negates itself with all the inevitability of a natural law. However, let capitalist private property disappear and its place be taken by public ownership, and the social problem is duly solved, for at one leap the proletariat passes from the realm of necessity into that of freedom. The social problem is said no longer to arise in the new state of public ownership of the means of production.

Nowadays we are in a position to compare these theses with reality. We can judge by the two different types of experiment with central controls carried out in Germany : firstly, controls *without* abolition of private property over the twelve year period 1936–48 ; secondly, controls *with* abolition of private ownership of the means of production, as in East Germany since 1945. We can establish point by point how the workers' situation has changed under a policy of central control in Germany. There are three aspects I wish to em-

phasize : firstly, supply deficiencies ; secondly, inequality of distribution ; and, lastly, insecurity.

(1) Advocates of central planning argue that manpower and the means of production will be more concentrated on supplying the working class once interest,
investment income, and unearned increment generally
have fallen away. Thus workers' needs are to receive
an increasing measure of satisfaction at the expense
of unearned increment. German experience, however,
has shown that central planners in fact gave priority
to increased investment, that is, to the rapid expansion
of the apparatus of production in industry, trade and
agriculture. The phenomen of forced saving is known
to economists. It can be induced by expanding credit
in a free economy : but it assumes far greater proportions in a planned economy, where investment is
forced by withdrawing productive forces as far as
possible from the manufacture of consumers' goods—
with the result that supplies to the working class sink
to a minimum level. The plans of German central
planning offices were plainly not aimed in the first
place at a maximum supply of consumers' goods.

Another point proved in Germany was that central
planning is incapable of realizing the principle of costs
in controlling the economy. (I shall have something
to say later on this subject, which I have discussed
more fully in an article in *Economica*, 1949.) The
forcing of investment by central planning authorities
and their inability to achieve a rational regulation of
production were the two factors that combined, in
Germany, to keep down the supply of goods to the
workers.

(2) In all types of free economy it is the price
mechanism that determines income levels. Critics
assail this on the grounds that it subordinates human
welfare to a blind mechanical process. It is said that
" fair shares " can only be achieved by central planning.

But German experience confirms the old truth that

distribution can be particularly unequal and unjust where economic power is concentrated and, besides, bound up with administrative power. This has often been the case in history—for example, take the late Roman Empire or the grave social crisis in thirteenth-century Flanders, or eighteenth-century landlordism. The dependence of income levels on market conditions can, as we have already pointed out, lead to grave injustice and certainly poses a considerable problem ; but no less dangerous is dependence on state officials who are called upon to carry out large scale investment programmes in addition to their normal functions.

The danger is further increased when these officials also administer public property, as is now the case in Eastern Germany. When that happens, all workers and other employees become dependent on a single owner of the means of production. They lose all freedom. At the same time the whole social structure is altered by the disappearance of independent farmers, artisans, etc. The association of central economic control with collective property represents a type of economic system that, judging by German experience, can be socially the most dangerous of all.

(3) It is now usual to regard security and freedom as antithetical. Security is said to require a renunciation of freedom. Modern man is believed to be more or less indifferent to freedom. What he wants above all is security. So the future belongs to central controls since that is the policy standing for security.

But German experience has shown that the antithesis between security and freedom does not exist at all. Let me give you an example. A metallurgical worker is ordered one evening by a central planning office to be at another town the next morning in order to assist in the building of a rolling mill. Should he fail to report at the stipulated time, he is threatened with penalties, sometimes even including forfeit of ration cards. Here we have *deprivation* of freedom of movement, of free choice of employment, of freedom of contract, and of consumers' freedom ; and deprivation of these liberties is just what causes insecurity. The man in question has long been in a position of being forced to do what he did not want to do. Previously—say, in 1931—he was dependent on an anonymous economic process. Then he lost his job without being able to find another for a long time. That was one form of insecurity. In 1940 he became dependent on officials who controlled his destiny. Once again he was insecure. One risk had been eliminated, only to be replaced by another ; for security presupposes the possession by the individual of liberty and choice of action.

Here our analysis of German experience penetrates to the heart of the social problem—freedom. It was lack of freedom that gave rise to frustration. The hegemony of private or public concentrations of power endangered the rule of justice, and lack of security arose from lack of freedom. Yet central control is bound to restrict liberty in the interests of planning, for the economy is not steered by the plans of individual households or firms, but by the central planning authorities who, willy-nilly, have been compelled by the inner logic of their system to adopt every method of directing labour in order to reach their targets.

Under the influence of Marxist ideas, it was often said in Germany that central controls might perhaps have economic disadvantages, but that socially they were good and necessary. Just the opposite has proved to be the case. It so happens that the social consequences of this type of economic control have turned out to be highly dangerous.

Reviewing German experience as a whole, we find the social problem taking three different forms in the course of the last half century. The problem of unfair shares, or inequality, was in the forefront up to the first world war. In the 'twenties and 'thirties the emphasis shifted to unemployment, its remedies and prevention. The third period, which began in the mid-'thirties, gave rise to a new social problem of unprecedented dimensions. Though insecurity in the form of unemployment had been eliminated, the concentration of power in the hands of central planning offices or of huge public concerns had engendered fresh insecurity, fresh injustice and supply shortages. The social problem, that had seemed to be approaching a solution early in the century, had become greater than ever.

This brings me back to the policy of full employment. In this connection I may be pardoned for relating some personal experiences. In September 1931, shortly before the devaluation of the pound, I took part in a two-day meeting at which President Luther of the Reichsbank was in the chair. The meeting discussed the gravely critical situation and the question whether the policy of deflation pursued hitherto should be replaced by one of state-created employment, low interest rates and expanding credit. My friends and I recommended this change of policy in view of the appalling situation at that time, when there were some five million unemployed. One of my friends declared that to continue the existing policy of contracting credit would not only entail the fall of the President of the Reichsbank, the Reich Chancellor and the government then in power, but also the end of the Republic. It must be obvious that, if there are millions of unemployed, any government will have to pursue a policy of full employment. Modern historical conditions compel it to do so. We must accept this as a fact. Social conscience forbids us to tolerate mass unemployment, and so does reason of state. That is one aspect of the matter, but there is another.

Our experiences in Germany show that a full employment policy does indeed establish full employment,

E

but it also leads in due course to unusual social and economic dangers. In Germany, the full employment policy partially stabilized the labour markets, that is, it eliminated mass unemployment. At the same time, however, it caused instability in foreign exchange markets and in numerous commodity markets ; and this in its turn created new economic problems, such as tensions in the foreign exchange markets and shortages of consumers' and producers' goods. The evil of unemployment was replaced by the evil of supply shortages. Over and above this, central planning led to a degree of social dependence without precedent in nineteenth- and twentieth-century Germany.

Thus our review of German experience leads us to a grave and serious conclusion. Economic policy is faced with a dilemma : on the one hand, mass unemployment necessitates a full employment policy ; on the other, the policy of full employment makes for an instability on other markets, which is extremely dangerous, and, in addition, forces economic policy in the direction of central planning. *This dilemma is perhaps the most crucial economic and social problem of our time.* Are we not obliged to pursue a policy of full employment ? Yet in doing so, are we not pursuing an economic policy whose economic and social consequences will in the long run prove intolerable ? Though the one social evil, unemployment, was eliminated in Germany, the price of that achievement was the establishment of a profoundly anti-social economic order. So what should we do ?

Before attempting to answer this crucial question, let us first remember this : the mass unemployment of the world crisis did not result from the inevitable development of " Capitalism," but rather from the existence of intrinsically unstable market forms and monetary systems.

We have been considering the German case in point from various angles, and we have seen that it was monopolies and oligopolies that gave rise to unstable markets. There was instability in the labour market and in many important commodity markets—for example, coal and iron. It was, however, the forms of money supply that had particularly harmful effects. By being completely bound up with the granting of credit, the supply of money reached a high degree of instability and was no longer co-ordinated with the price system. When prices fell, money contracted further, and so on indefinitely, the fall in prices causing contraction of money and a further fall in prices. This is not the case with all monetary systems, but it was so with the system prevailing in particular after the first world war. It can be firmly established that unstable market forms and monetary systems are bound to lead to cumulative depression and mass unemployment. This being so, economic policy should concentrate on developing systems conducive to market equilibrium, and in this respect the configuration of the monetary system is particularly important. The essential aim of economic and social policy should be to construct a framework for the everyday functioning of the economy, and not to attempt sole control of the economy by means of central planning. For to do so will make it impossible to preserve freedom as well, and without freedom there can be no solution to the economic problem. Before the great crisis of 1929–32, economic policy engendered market forms and monetary systems which lacked equilibrium, and this found expression in mass unemployment. The policy of full employment eliminated unemployment but increased the instability of other markets, with consequences already familiar to us. The time has now come to dig deeper, as it were, and attend generally to the development of systems which will prevent disturbances ot equilibrium. The policy of full employment will then no longer be necessary and the great dilemma will have been overcome.

Those who visit Germany to-day will notice no little scepticism in many quarters about the policy of full employment. This also surprises the Military Government experts. Such scepticism does not arise, as one might think, from deficient social sense, but is the outcome of experience since 1933. Touring Germany in 1946, a British expert of standing noted an unusual degree of economic stress and shortage of supply among the population *despite* full employment. Such experiences affect the German attitude. There is no question of return to *laissez-faire*, but the policy of full employment is inadequate. It is not enough merely to restore equilibrium to the labour market. But the achievement of general equilibrium requires the establishment of certain market forms and monetary systems ; and this is the primary task of economic policy.

IV

MONETARY POLICY AND ITS CONSEQUENCES

THE history of German currency during the last half century is a dramatic one. The period on the gold standard, lasting until 1914, was followed by two great inflations between 1914 and 1923, and between 1936 and 1948. Both these inflations were concluded by a reform of the currency, which in each case was successful. Between 1929 and 1932 there was a severe deflation which set a different type of problem.

The effects of these varying experiments with monetary policy are all but incalculable. Surveying them inclines one to the opinion of those historiographers who believe not only economics, but all history, to be essentially determined by the behaviour of money. The inflations, for instance, had quite revolutionary effects on the social structure in Germany. Whole strata of the middle class were destroyed by them. At the same time they aggravated the problem of " social security " which, as we know, has in modern times come increasingly to the fore in all economic and social policy. By losing most of their savings on two occasions, German workers, other employees, and the rest, found their social security greatly diminished. This is a fact of quite fundamental importance to any consideration of the present-day social problem in Germany. There was much talk of social security in those years, but less was done. It was particularly the policy of inflation that diminished social security.

If now we are to attempt a more precise investigation of the effects of German monetary policy during the last half century, we find that the complexity of phenomena compels us to limit our scope. There are,

however, three major questions which arise in this
connection, and I hope that discussion of them will
serve to illuminate important general principles.

Firstly, let us discuss the connection between monetary policy and the structure of the economic order.
Then, let us consider the effect of monetary policy on
international trade. And lastly, let us analyze monetary policy in relation to counter-measures against
depressions and crises.

Let us begin with the deflationary policy pursued
between 1929 and 1932. This deflation led to a general
recession of demand, or, more precisely, to a shift in
the demand curves. Whereas certain prices, above
all monopoly prices, remained relatively firm, others
changed rapidly. Assets shrank with the depreciation
of machines, stocks, etc., while liabilities remained
constant. We can express this in more general terms
by saying that the mark failed as a medium of exchange
and was at the same time no longer an adequate unit
of account. So, deflation rendered the German price
system less capable of controlling everyday economic
processes. Losses in business calculations of costs, or
balances, arose to a large extent from the deflation.
The losses, for example, of a weaving or shoe-making
factory did not indicate with any certainty whether
or not there had been mismanagement of labour and
material means of production at any particular point ;
for the loss in question might merely have been the
outcome of deflation. Business accounting thus became
in part meaningless.

It is interesting to note the reaction of German
economic policy to deflation. Instead of eliminating
the *cause* of depression—the deflation itself—an attempt
was made to eliminate the *effects*. An important example
in this connection is the German agricultural policy of
the time, especially as it can be regarded as a precursor
of planned influencing of the market in many other
countries of the world. Between 1929 and 1932,

falling agricultural prices led to price manipulations designed to guarantee the farmer a definite price or a definite income. The main points of this agricultural policy were : reduction of imports ; so-called market controls to keep German agricultural prices above the crisis level of the world market ; and subsidies, in that the state bought up bread grain and supplied it cheaply as fodder. This agricultural policy was generally successful. The proceeds from the sale of agricultural products are vitally dependent on the incomes of the consumers. There can be no doubting this after the vicissitudes of the world crisis, nor does it apply to Germany alone. Propping up agricultural prices was quite unable to eliminate the effects of diminishing demand for agricultural products. Statistics show that the proceeds of agricultural sales continued to decline with further deflation and shrinking of consumers' income, e.g. working-class incomes. Measures in the agricultural sector alone could not successfully counter-act the effects of deflationary crisis. General methods of monetary policy were required—in other words, the overcoming of deflation itself.

Agricultural policy, however, had considerable reper-cussions on the rest of German economic policy, in particular, on trade policy ; for the previous system of trade agreements was destroyed by the new agricultural policy—though, indeed, by no means by this alone. Deflation provoked, amongst other things, a new agricultural policy and a new autarchic trade policy. Such was the situation until 1932 when deflation finally engendered a counter-stroke in the form of a powerful impulse towards full employment.

Like other European countries, Germany has more experience of inflation than of deflation. We Germans underwent a major open inflation from 1914 to 1923 and a major suppressed inflation from 1936 to 1948. Both, but especially the latter, vitally influenced the structure of the economic order. Here again the complexity of phenomena compels us to concentrate on particular points. It is to be emphasized in the first place that inflation robbed the price mechanism of its power to direct the economic process adequately. Prices rose unevenly. For example, rents or the prices of certain raw materials remained behind while other prices rose rapidly. Business calculation of costs thus became inaccurate, since price relationships no longer reflected scarcity relationships. This was the case with the open inflation between 1914 and 1923 ; but suppressed inflation, which consists in pegging prices while expanding money, immediately puts the price system out of action, for alterations of data are no longer visible in the prices. Price loses its selective function when all commodities can find a market.

By robbing the price system of its ability to control the economic process adequately, the inflations prompted the adoption of a different method of control, namely, central planning. This was what happened in the housing market, for example. In both inflations, rents were controlled for social reasons, and since inflationary pressure drove demand far above supply, rooms and dwellings had to be rationed. Thus a system of central allocation of dwellings became established. Particularly important, however, was the pegging of foreign exchange rates during the second big inflation which was, of course, a suppressed inflation. A lack of equilibrium immediately became evident in the foreign exchange markets, necessitating central allocation of foreign exchange. Allocations were not only made in respect of certain groups of commodities which were to be imported, as for instance cotton, wool, copper, nickel, etc., but also in respect of individual firms receiving these raw materials. The firms had to be selected and their production programmes examined. Should this spinning mill receive cotton ? If so, how much ? That was the sort of question the authorities had to decide, and they could only do so if there was a certain central plan governing the economic process as a whole. So the mid-thirties already saw the foreign exchange market injecting a considerable element of central planning into the German economic system. Suppressed inflation was not the only reason for the establishment of a planned economy, but it was an important factor and a precondition.

This brings us to another point. Not only did the inflations destroy the price system and hence all free types of economic order, not only did they engender or decisively foster the tendency to central planning, but they were also a precondition of the existence of central planning. Appreciation of this interconnection is one of the most important fruits of German experience in the field of economic policy. In time of suppressed inflation, businesses and households have considerable cash holdings. Hence, businesses can comply with restrictions on the use of stocks, with production directives and prohibitions of the sale of goods. They can still afford wages and pay for new allocations of raw materials, just because their cash holdings are so large. But when money becomes scarce, as it did after the 1948 Currency Reform, businesses have to sell stocks of finished goods, etc., in order to maintain production and to avoid closing down and causing unemployment. A leather factory, for instance, had to sell leather in order to keep going. It also processed impounded hides to enable it to make further sales and so currently earn the money needed for maintenance of production. Central planning—in the leather business, for instance—was thus rendered impossible. Scarcity of money, as it were, exploded the planned economy. A surplus of money is a precondition of central planning just as, conversely, scarce money is a hindrance to it. There is a further or second reason why this should be so. So long as households dispose of plenty of cash, they buy all the goods coming into the market—irrespective of quality.

But as soon as they have less cash, consumers choose very carefully. Goods such as substitute foodstuffs, shoes, etc., manufactured according to the specifications of the central planning authorities, can then no longer be marketed and find a ready sale. A proportion remains unsold. The consumer begins to regain influence over the economic process.

This tendency has become very evident in Germany since the 1948 Currency Reform. A great many goods of inferior quality are no longer marketable. As money grows scarce, control of the economic process necessarily shifts to the consumer, and the central planning authorities lose power. Control of the economic process changes hands. Household and business planning gains influence. Planned economy, on the other hand, correlates with inflation.

The picture will become more complete as we investigate the second complex of problems presented by monetary policy and international trade.

First, a short preliminary remark about the inflation from 1914 to 1923. Responsibility for the monetary catastrophe was at that time often attributed to the so-called adverse German balance of payments. It was maintained that the excessive influx of goods increased demand for foreign exchange, raised exchange rates, sent up the price of imported raw materials—for example, cotton or copper—and so compelled monetary expansion. Thus the balance of payments was thought to determine the quantity of money. In reality the contrary was true—and this is not without interest to-day. The real connection was that prices and exchange rates rose as a result of the budgetary deficit and so affected German international trade. Furthermore, it was monetary policy that largely determined the balance of payments, and not *vice versa*. That this was the true connection was proved by the facts of the great currency reform in 1923–24. Less interesting nowadays, but important in principle, was

the effect of German deflationary policy from 1929 to
1932. It greatly improved the balance of trade, but
was accompanied by a considerable fall in the standard
of living and increased unemployment. At that time,
in 1931, Germany achieved an export surplus of 3,000
million marks.

More relevant to-day are the consequences for
international trade of the inflationary policy after 1933.
The very fact that exchange rates were pegged and
the state henceforth compelled to control imports, and
later exports as well, made foreign exchange policy
more and more into a trade policy. Indeed, foreign
exchange policy may be said to be a far more effective
instrument for influencing a country's international
trade than trade policy.

These observations, however, merely scratch the
surface of the facts. We must carry our analysis rather
deeper ; and German experiments give us every
incentive to do so.

In view of the somewhat academic nature of the discussion, it is necessary at this point to call certain
concrete facts and questions to mind. At a German
frontier station, we see goods trains laden with machinery
leaving the country, and train loads of leather or textile
raw materials entering it. Each exported machine is
lost to the country as a direct source of goods supply.
Conversely, each imported piece of leather or bale of
cotton represents an increase in the supply of goods.
But what check is there on whether each individual
machine leaving the country and exchanged for leather
is not of greater utility to the population than the
imported leather ? Exact calculations should be made
for each individual commodity and not only for individual types of commodity. What needs to be
determined is the value of each exported commodity
and of each imported commodity from the point of
view of supplying the population. An exact " calculating machine " is required for the solution of this

problem, which is set innumerable times daily. If it is *not* solved, foreign trade is inadequately controlled from the economic point of view. Goods are exported which should not be exported, and *vice versa. Foreign trade loses point without an exact calculating machine*, since it depends in the first place on the selection of manifold individual commodities.

We have seen this happen in Germany. We were saying that controls were introduced into the exchange market in the 'thirties. It was left to the central planning offices to carry out allocations of foreign exchange in respect of individual goods. Of course they could only make general estimates. They could not know whether single bales of cotton or single tons of iron ore were really so urgently required as other commodities which could not be imported. But exchange control was only the beginning. The fixing of foreign exchange prices necessitated state stimulation of exports in order to increase exchange holdings. This was done by means of the Additional Exports Scheme whereby certain subsidies were given to businesses engaged in exports. The greater the influence gained by central planning within the framework of the German economic system, the more it devolved upon the central planning offices to decide what goods were exported, and the less success was achieved in determining whether the selection of individual types and quantities of goods for export corresponded to the aims of the central planners or to the needs of the population. What was lacking was the calculating machine that could determine this. Let us beware of " global " estimates in this connection. It is not a question of encouraging certain " export industries " and of restricting the import of certain classes of goods. The real question is rather how far each single commodity leaving the country can be correctly valued, and how by doing this a foundation can be laid on which to build up a rational foreign trade. Export and import figures have little significance unless they reflect a rational economic accounting which can be used to calculate the precise degree of scarcity of individual goods.   Hence the encouragement of so-called " export industries " in Germany not seldom proved abortive.   The prior problem is to select which businesses should export and import, and which goods may economically be exported and which imported.   So long as economic calculations failed to select adequately, all stimulation of exports was mere groping in the dark.   Nor do I believe that certain " global " estimates, for example of import or export elasticity, do justice to reality.   The important thing is to determine to what extent individual commodities contribute to the overcoming of scarcity.

The relevant problem is now becoming evident on the international plane.   There is, for instance, the problem of investment control in various countries. How far should the Dutch iron industry be developed, how far the German, Italian and French iron industries ?   Which works should be enlarged and what special plant constructed ?   So long as there is no exact and internationally valid ready-reckoner, it is plainly impossible to answer the question, for no one knows the optimum location of individual branches of industry, or their optimum size in individual countries, and while the various countries lack a uniform ready-reckoner, there can be no exact comparison of production costs in individual areas—such as the Ruhr and the industrial region of Northern France.

So we come to the conclusion that both the foreign trade of individual countries, and international trade as a whole, stand in need of the old practical ready-reckoner.   The destruction of this by deflations and above all by inflations, for instance in the form of suppressed inflation, cut the ground from under the feet of Germany's international trade and that of other countries.   Adequate internal accounting and the establishment of an international unit of account are

questions which have priority over all discussions about
protection and free trade, and indeed over all trade
policy. The problem is not rightly envisaged if, for
instance, one seeks to show that exchange rates only
partially affected the prices of goods. What really
matters is the internal economic accounting of countries
and the exchange rate which has the function of aligning
the various price systems.

What we have learnt in Germany is this very fact,
that without economic accounting and an international
unit of account, we cannot again achieve international
division of labour in the exchange of goods and the
development of investment.

This brings us to German experiences in connection
with the problem of monetary and trade cycle policy.
The preliminary to modern trade cycle policy is anxiety
about the investment gap. It is thought that the
inevitable course of capitalist evolution gives rise to
the investment gap. Hence the demand for, and the
adoption of, a policy of low interest rates.

There undoubtedly was an investment gap in Germany in the period between 1929 and 1932, and the
consequences were in fact those known to us from
textbooks : namely, deficient demand, even in consumers' goods industries and agriculture. But, if we
enquire after the causes of the investment gap at that
time and seek an answer in realities rather than in
textbooks, we find the following : apart from the
deterrent effect of falling prices on the incentive to
invest, there were two circumstances in particular
that deterred entrepreneurs from investment. First
came the relationship of costs to prices. If, say, the
prices of production goods were kept high by cartels,
or if wages were fixed by state intervention, the result
could be price relationships that made investment seem
pointless. In the crisis year, 1931, Berlin builders, for
instance, had to reckon with certain relatively firm
prices of materials, such as iron and cement, which

were fixed by syndicates, and also with relatively fixed wages, where housing prices were dropping rapidly. If only for this reason, the incentive to build houses became very slight. Here again the fundamental fact made itself felt that the economic process—in this case investment—is only adequately governed by prices when price relationships correctly reflect scarcity relationships.

There is also a second consideration of equal importance. A certain constancy of individual economic data is necessary if large-scale investments are to be planned. For instance, a manufacturer considering whether he should enlarge his engineering factory would abandon the project if he feared a swift change in taxation or a sudden devaluation in other countries. The remarkable instability of the experimental economic policy carried out in Germany and most other industrial countries increased the element of risk to such an extent that the incentive to invest was seriously diminished. Lack of constancy is an important characteristic of economic policy in the Age of Experiment that began in 1914. Usually it is greatly underestimated. The volume of investment also depends to a significant degree on the constancy or inconstancy of economic policy.

To sum up : investments rapidly declined at that time, because with falling prices calculations of costs made investment seem unprofitable and because risks were increased by rapid alternations of economic policy.

In this case too, economic policy behaved as it so often does ; instead of eliminating the *causes* of the damage—here, those of the investment gap—it counteracted the effects. Monetary policy was used to make the damage disappear. In general, it is very typical of the age of experimental monetary policy that disproportion should first of all have been caused in the price system by the formation of pressure groups in

industry, agriculture and labour, and by the introduction of a very unstable monetary system, and so on.
Then, after the event, monetary policy was given the
task of clearing up the damage done. In any case,
that was what happened in Germany, as we have seen
in Chapter III. We also know that these methods
succeeded in eliminating unemployment. So the
policy of cheap money proved itself in this respect.

But that was not the whole story. As unemployment
disappeared a different kind of disproportion became
evident. The investments set in motion with the help
of the policy of low interests rates and state-created
employment, were not attuned to one another. For
example, a great many motor roads were built ; but
the utility of those roads was in many cases slight,
because supplies of petrol and motor transport could
not be correspondingly increased. So, in general, this
trade cycle policy lacked the instrument for bringing
the individual parts of the economic process into
equilibrium with one another, which was the only way
to effect a commensurate increase in supplies. It then
became evident in Germany that the modern industrialized economy is subject to two types of economic
disturbance. In the first instance, industrial and
agricultural enterprises lack markets, which gives rise
to unemployment, machinery stands idle and stocks
accumulate. That the economy is out of control is
plain for all to see. The second type of disturbance
has gained ground particularly during the last decade.
It is one in which, though all factors are engaged, human
activities are not properly co-ordinated and investments
are not in line with one another, with the result that
bottlenecks form. Under-employment characterizes
the first type, which is often chronic. An example of
the former was the German situation between 1929
and 1932 with unemployment figures running into
millions. The latter was exemplified by the situation
from 1938 to 1948 with full employment and rapidly

diminishing supplies. Monetary policy, in particular the policy of cheap money, may well have eliminated the one evil, but only to engender the other.

In conclusion, let us take the German position between 1945 and 1948. It represents a border-line case and is, for that reason, of particular interest. The situation was characterized by the destruction of numerous economic enterprises and by a shortage of raw materials everywhere. Much of this was directly due to the war, but there was a further symptom worthy of special attention, namely, that even existing possibilities of production were insufficiently exploited. For instance, crowds flocked daily into the countryside to barter for food. Millions of working hours per day were lost in this way. All these people could undoubtedly have found far more productive use for their labour power, for the factories were at that time crying out for labour. What was the explanation? Suppressed inflation had rendered the price system incapable of controlling the economy. There was no adequate unit of account, nor were essential goods, especially food and raw materials, to be bought for money. Free economic forms were out of action ; and so were the central planning offices, for they could not usefully co-ordinate available labour forces and means of production. Since all possible methods of steering a large-scale economy involving division of labour had clearly broken down, there arose quite primitive forms of economy, such as barter and growing food in home gardens, that circumvented any comprehensive division of labour. Thus a great industrialized country developed an economic system equivalent to conditions in the time of Charlemagne. Once this has been understood, it is easy to grasp why the Currency Reform would prove so effective, and why production and supply rose by leaps and bounds afterwards. The reform reinstated an adequate unit of account, enabled control of the economy by prices, and gave rise to forms of economic

F

order providing a framework for the organization of large-scale division of labour.

Experience has, however, confirmed the primacy of monetary policy not only in this case, but in all economic policy during the last decades. " The destruction of bourgeois society is brought about by the devastation of its monetary system." There is a considerable element of truth in this remark of Lenin's, despite its demagogic flavour. Conversely one can say that only when money is adjusted to the balance mechanism of the economic process, does it become possible to attain general equilibrium by means of the price system.

V

DEVELOPMENT OF ECONOMIC THOUGHT

ECONOMIC thought is a political force. It determines and orientates economic and political action. Moreover, it is a power in its own right, and not, as Marx thought, just a reflex of prevailing economic and social conditions. Certain fundamental convictions, such as the belief that economic policy inevitably develops central planning, are formative historical forces.

It will help us to understand the present state of economic thought in Germany if we look back briefly into the past as far as the eighteen-seventies. German economic science then aspired to comprehend economic realities more fully than the classical economists had done. This aspiration which led to greater realism also gave rise to a schism of economic thought in German-speaking lands. Menger, in Austria, led an attempt at renewed theoretical analysis of primary economic facts. There emerged the Marginal Utility School of world-wide significance. In Germany, however, research took a different turning under Schmoller's leadership. Stress was laid on the description of individual facts. In Schmoller's own words : " economic science should mainly proceed descriptively, collect empirical material, solve individual problems and only then, basing itself on such facts, go on to formulate a theory." This programme was carried out in earnest. Innumerable descriptions were carefully worked out for individual branches of economy, such as the iron and steel industry, agriculture in the various regions and valleys of Germany, and so on. The leaders of this historical school hoped eventually to advance from the complexity of individual descriptions to a general description which they called " theory." The rejection of theoretical analysis in favour of collecting facts was *one* characteristic of the historical school. Another was the view, expressed by Schmoller as follows : " Modern research, and civilized nations generally, now largely believe in the progress and unity of human evolution. We set out from this belief." The idea of evolution, and in particular of inevitable historical evolution, governed the thinking of the historical school.

After the eighteen-seventies, these fundamental principles of research also became increasingly influential in the sphere of practical economics and politics ; for the economic and political attitude of the historical school was just as *ad hoc* as its descriptive method of scholarship. The idea was lost sight of, that all economic phenomena are interrelated and hence that there exists a general interdependence of economic processes. Social policy, as we already know, therefore took the form of proposing and executing isolated measures, such as workers' insurance. At the same time economic policy again and again expressed the idea that new economic developments represent progress and should be welcomed. For example, the cartels, which had been spreading rapidly since the beginning of the century, were accepted on the grounds that they were the outcome of a necessary process of historical evolution. The historical school and the Marxists thought alike in this respect.

Description of individual facts, avoidance of fundamental decisions, *ad hoc* economic and social measures, faith in the necessity of historical evolution—all this characterized the fundamental attitude of the historical school, which determined the thought and action of succeeding generations in Germany. A certain opposition was, of course, never entirely lacking. There were individuals like Heinrich Dietzel who carried on the classical tradition ; and the opposition also reflected the influence of modern Austrian and English theory. But the historical school prevailed.

It is desirable to view the further developments of German economic thought against this background. The historical school indeed survives, but no longer prevails. It has been contradicted by other economic thinking on different lines, and it is this change in economic thought that we must discuss now.

The change was in part brought about by historical events themselves. The first world war, and particularly the inflation, set problems that the historical school was unable to solve. Many descriptions of a monetary historical type were made, and an account was given of earlier inflations, for example those of the American Civil War or of the French Revolution ; but no theory was available to explain the interrelationship of facts. Hence it was no coincidence that the first inflation, for example, was not understood and the currency decline wrongly explained, and that no timely remedies were possible. The problems set by reality were more than could be coped with by the economic science of the time. Not only monetary problems were involved, but also general problems of economic system arising from cartelization, socialization, etc.

Of course, it was by no means historical facts alone that demanded a change of economic thought. The origins of the change lie deeper, and it would probably have taken place even without the failure of the historical school. The first decade of this century was particularly full of intellectual stirrings in Germany. People again became more concerned with fundamental issues, and appreciation of theoretical work increased.

To attempt to describe this change in German economic thought is a difficult task. There is no summing it up with a brief slogan such as " the Renaiscence of Theory." Moreover, within the narrow framework of this book, I must concentrate on bringing out the economic and political consequences of the new ways of thinking.

But, let me try to give the gist of the developments in methodology and theory, which fall into five main sections.

(1) An attempt was made to resolve the " great antinomy " of economic science. What does this mean ?

The interrelationships of the everyday economic process can, as we know, be explored by theoretical analysis, since the uniformity of everyday events provides scope for general theoretical treatment. Let us take the case of the man who saves. Saving raises important problems which cannot be clarified by mere statements of facts. If, for instance, we tried to observe the course of a saved ten pound note on its way into the bank and back again into production, we should soon be in a labyrinth and lose the thread. And if, by observing the retail trade and consumers' goods industry, we tried to ascertain the effects of the missing amount saved, we should also find ourselves in a maze. Since no solution is possible on those lines, economic science investigates the problem of saving *theoretically*. The complex of facts is taken to pieces and only one quantity is varied ; in other words, it is supposed that only saving takes place, everything else remaining the same. Thus our duty to explain the concrete economic process in its general context has entailed and entails theoretical work.

There is, however, another aspect to economic reality. Human economy is constantly changing its forms. Political, legal and social institutions, and human convictions and tastes, are subject to historical change, and the everyday economy changes with them. The effects of that man's saving in, say, the England of 1920, would have been different in 1931 and different again in 1946. It means one thing nowadays for a Russian to save and quite another for an American.

What is true of this example is true generally. The steering of the everyday economic process varies according to the type of economic system. The doubt then arises whether it is in any way possible to comprehend the economy in its entirety, in view of this continual flux of economic forms. Does not the historical nature of the economy preclude the application of theoretical methods of thought in our field of study? With this question we find ourselves caught up in the fundamental antinomy of economics, which has deeply engaged, and still engages, the attention of economists, in particular German economists. Economic science must proceed from the individual and historical manifold nature of its subject matter, otherwise the ground is cut away from under its feet. But it can only solve its problems and comprehend reality as a complex whole by setting out those problems in a general form and thus making them susceptible of theoretical investigation. Economic science is compelled to do justice to the historical diversity of economic forms and yet, at the same time, to treat problems in a theoretical and general way.

The whole history of political economy could be written from this angle. The swing of the pendulum is everywhere apparent. If, in a country, theoretical analysis is pursued beyond the bounds of historical reality, a recoil follows and pure description gives place to statistics of historical fact. But when description has prevailed for a time, theoretical analysis gains ground again and the pendulum swings in the opposite direction. Economic reality is, however, never successfully comprehended in all its interrelationships, because no one has yet succeeded in fully co-ordinating historical and statistical experience with theoretical thought.

German economic science tried to solve this crucial problem by dispensing, first of all, with old, inexact and all-embracing terms like Socialism and Capitalism ; then, penetrating, as it were, into individual businesses and households, it attempted to overcome the antinomy by analyzing them. I think the attempt has succeeded. Underlying all economic diversity is the fundamental fact that all economic action proceeds from planning. Investigation of individual business planning, in the case of a farm for instance, and of how this planning arises, leads to the following results. In so far as the farm produces for its own consumption, it is a self-sufficient and centrally administered economy ; in so far as it buys and sells, it is a member of an economy of free exchange. Both are very intimately connected on the farm and form a unit. But economic science can discern two basic components that need to be distinguished in order to arrive at the two fundamental forms of economy : the centrally controlled economy and the free economy. A great deal more, however, can be discovered from this one farm. Traces of a different kind of centrally administered economy are, for example, to be found in the various restrictions, crop controls and delivery quotas complied with by the farm management. The farm business is here overshadowed by great, centrally controlled, economic structures under public authority, and is, in this respect, a member of a centralized administrative economy. At the same time it is possible to distinguish the many forms of free economy—market forms and monetary systems—encountered in this farm business, for example, the market forms of seller's monopoly, oligopoly, etc. If this method of investigation is extended to a large number of past and present economic units, we arrive at the important conclusion that a fusion of a limited number of pure economic forms is taking place in all concrete economy, such as in England to-day and in France at the end of the nineteenth century. Just as innumerable tunes can be constructed from a few notes, so innumerable economic systems are formed by the fusion of a limited number of pure forms. This enables precise definition and comparison of the structure of all economic systems in history, such as the English systems of 1950, 1900 or 1700, or the Russian of 1940. At the same time we obtain a firm basis for theoretical analysis, for we can now investigate the course of the economic process within the framework of individual pure forms capable of exact definition. Thus we are rid of the intolerable state of affairs where theoretical analysis has to be based on such vague terms as Capitalism or Socialism.

So, research has shown that morphological analysis of reality must precede theoretical work, if the antinomy between historical investigation and theoretical analysis is to be overcome. The exact definition of forms of economic system is the first task economics must perform in order to resolve the antithesis of theory and history and to gather scientific experience.

(2) Associated with this was the controversy about " historical inevitability." Most people think of Marx first in this connection—not altogether correctly. Marx developed the idea in a distinctive way, but it appeared earlier in a more universal form. We are most affected to-day by one of the earliest formulations ; I mean the famous Saint-Simonist Doctrine of 1829–30. Saint-Simon and his followers were inspired by the natural sciences to seek a law governing the historical process in the same way as the law of gravity governs nature, and they thought they had discovered it in the form of the " law of progress." They regarded mankind as a collective unity, progressing and evolving according to certain laws. Mankind, they said, must inevitably pass through certain phases of existence. " The Golden Age, hitherto set in the past by purblind tradition, lies before us " ; such was the vision of the Saint-Simonists. Marx had a different, though not dissimilar, vision. He prophesied the concentration of capital ; competition, he said, would kill itself because many capitalists would be expropriated by few ; and as the number of capitalist magnates progressively

diminished, there would be a corresponding increase in the measure of poverty, oppression and exploitation suffered by the working class. This was " the absolute and general law of capitalist accumulation " inevitably heading for crises and the final expropriation of the expropriators.

Belief in historical inevitability has now become a doctrine governing economic policy in most countries. So it is all the more important to question the existence of any such inevitability.

German economic science has been much pre-occupied with this problem, particularly in connection with the analysis of the forms of economic system dis-cussed under my first heading. Two points were established first :

(*a*) We know of no laws inevitably determining the course of history or of economic policy. As we have already seen, the elimination of competition and the development of monopoly in the modern world are by no means inevitable. The famous law of historical evolution proves to be an image, not of reality, but of the wishes of certain political economists.

(*b*) Schumpeter, who seeks to resurrect the old faith, once said that facts harbinger the future. This point of view would have us recognize in economic facts the shape of things to come. But this maxim is untenable in the face of history. Economic policy does not derive in the first instance from the economic facts, but from human opinions about the facts. So much experience teaches us. Speaking from his wealth of historical learning, Hecksher once said that " Economic policy is not so much determined by economic reality as by the conceptions of this reality existing in people's minds." Nowadays, for instance, it is more the principle of nationalism or the desire for security that has formed ideas about economic reality and thus decisively influenced economic policy—less so the economic facts themselves.

However, we have not yet solved the problem of inevitability. We can only do so by continuing at this stage to dispense with general slogans and penetrate instead into reality itself. Then we discover, for instance, that those who had a share in framing German economic policy between 1929 and 1933, felt strongly that the grave crisis virtually dictated certain economic measures of state. Similarly in other cases. Haphazard distribution would have seriously dislocated the processing industries if central allocation of iron and steel had not been introduced after the 1936 price-freeze. Central allocation and planning of iron and steel were virtually inevitable under the circumstances. Such situations often occur and suggest that there may, after all, be an element of inevitability in economic policy. Yet further investigation shows : (a) that, for example, the emergency situation from 1929 to 1933 may well have virtually compelled German economic policy to create unemployment, but that the constellation of circumstances dictating this policy was not a necessary one. The swift and fateful contraction of money was the outcome of a particular system of monetary supply ; and it is not necessary for money to be exclusively bound up with an unstable system of credit. Nor was it necessary to realize market forms lacking in equilibrium. Thus the tendency towards state creation of employment and expansion of credit arose from an unnecessary constellation of circumstances. (b) Secondly, even if a particular economic policy was indicated in this and other cases, there was nothing so very definite about what should be done in detail. Germany could, for instance, also have devalued the mark at the time of the British devaluation in September 1931. Such a step would have had far-reaching consequences for the whole economic and political development of the next decade.

From these observations may be drawn certain important conclusions regarding economic action.

Every act of economic policy needs to be considered from three aspects. Let us take the example of a protective tariff. In a predominantly competitive economic system, a tariff leads directly to an alteration in the supply of goods. Over and above this, it can give rise to a tendency towards monopoly formation in the protected industry and thereby initiate a change in the economic system. Once the formation of monopoly has been completed, say, in the iron and steel industry, it may affect other systems, for instance the political order, since monopolies can gain influence over legislation. So we see that the impression of inevitability prevailing at the moment of any given act of economic policy, is in fact often to blame for its own existence.

Great thinkers of the past have again and again come upon the fact that man, with one freely taken step, finds himself entangled and is no longer free. As Goethe says : " The first is freedom ; the second, bondage." Analysis of modern economic and political realities confirms this old truth. Once recognized, however, it enables economic policy to set conditions of a general political order that preclude unwanted tendencies.

(3) Some twenty years ago, the idea prevailed in Germany that the inevitable trend of history was away from " capitalism " towards central planning. It was thought that the policy of *laissez-faire* had come to an end because, together with capitalism, it had led to " anarchy of production," and that the development of great monopoly formations necessitated a transition to central planning. Rockefeller, Carnegie, Stinnes, and their like, were regarded as precursors of central planning. The step from private monopoly to a policy of central planning was inevitable, and the important thing was to devise central planning as efficiently and humanely as possible. This was the task of the future. There was no choice between *laissez-faire* and central

planning, and no sense in rejecting central planning ; the problem was how best to organize it.

This ideology has now been largely discarded in Germany as a result of economic and political experience gathered during the last decades and of developments in economic thought.

This is due in the first place to criticism of *laissez-faire* and central planning having been carried very much further than previously. Slogans, such as " anarchy of production," etc., are not sufficient criticism of *laissez-faire* and of so-called Capitalism. Thorough investigation of the forms of system realized in the *laissez-faire* period reveals varying degrees of efficiency. Certain market forms—for example, bilateral monopolies, oligopolies, etc.—or certain monetary systems, such as the linking up of money and credit, do lack equilibrium ; but other market forms and monetary systems are far more efficient. The fact that the price system in the *laissez-faire* period was not in perfect running order does not mean that the price system is quite incapable of governing the economic process. What experience of *laissez-faire* goes to prove is that the economic *system* cannot be left to organize itself. So there is no question of any return to *laissez-faire*.

At the same time, criticisms of central planning, henceforth based on considerable experience, indicated that a centrally administered economy lacks an adequate unit of account, is unable to make exact calculations of costs, and is socially dangerous by reason of the concentration of power involved. People have laughed at the old faith in the harmony of interests that found expression in the policy of *laissez-faire*. It has since been learnt that the new doctrine of harmonized interests in central planning is equally odd.

Criticism of *laissez-faire* and central planning has shown that people are under no compulsion to adopt the very dangerous policy of central planning. On the contrary, economic policy could of its own accord

check the development of monopoly, industrial concentration, etc., and thereby bring into play the considerable forces engendered by modern technology.
Encouragement could be given to market forms and
monetary systems making for a competitive price
system. All sectors of economic policy—laws of liability
or of banking, or trade policy—could aim at establishing
conditions in industrial economy favourable to the
organization of an efficient and humane economic
system. Such an economic policy would not first let
things slide into a state of monopoly and monetary
disequilibrium, and *then* proceed to centralize control
of the everyday economic process.

(4) With this change in German economic thinking,
went a critical rejection of the *ad hoc* type of economic
policy. The historical school which, as I have mentioned, still survives in Germany as a ramification of
economic thought, neglected to give due consideration
to the interrelationship of all economic facts and therefore to the interdependence in their effects of all individual measures of economic policy. The essential
problem of economic policy is now seen to be the
question of how to provide adequate guidance, with a
uniform unit of account, for the modern, large-scale,
economic process based on division of labour. From
this point of view, German economists are now, under-
standably, somewhat sceptical about any trade cycle
policy that lets itself be stampeded by a temporary
emergency into impeding or stopping the functioning
of the price system—for example, by foreign exchange
control, state-fostered expansion of credit, or other
measures of the kind. It is equally illegitimate for fiscal
policy, for example, to tax business in such a way as
to stimulate the process of concentration and thus favour
the growth of monopoly. Modern economy is a vast
system of interrelationships. All acts of economic
policy therefore affect the economic process as a whole
and should be attuned to one another. General prin-

ciples of economic order need to be developed and acted on, in order to assure the unity of economic policy.

But the possibilities of providing adequate guidance for the industrialized economic process are seen to be limited. There are economic systems in which central planning authorities control the economic process, and there are others in which the plans and decisions of many businesses and households mainly determine the economic process. Obviously, the latter methods of free economic control vary greatly according to whether the economic units are, or are not, combined in monopolistic or similar groups. Roughly speaking, we can distinguish three methods of control applicable to the industrialized economic process : control by central state authorities, by groups, and by competition. Analysis of German experience strongly suggests that, given an adequate monetary system, control by competition is far superior to both the other methods.

(5) Our experience also provides an answer to the question whether the state should do more or less. "*Less*," say the advocates of *laissez-faire* ; " *more*," cry the central planners. Friends of compromise solutions seek a middle way. They would like the state to plan and, at the same time, to give scope for private planning and initiative.

But the problem needs to be stated differently if it is to be solved. The question whether there should be more or less state activity evades the essential issue which relates to quality, not quantity. In our age of industry, modern technology, cities and masses, it is clearly intolerable that the economic system should be left to organize itself. It is clear also that the state is equally incapable of regulating the everyday process of so complex an economy based on division of labour. What, therefore, should be the nature of state activity ? The answer is that the state should influence the *forms* of economy, but not itself direct the economic process.

Concluding trade treaties, providing for an adequate monetary system, framing laws of patent and contract—all this lies within the purview of the state. The state should also decide the general nature of the economic and political order and thus meaningfully integrate the various sectors of economic policy ; but it should not take upon itself the issue of production orders regluating the day-to-day manufacture, import and export of machines, textiles, wheat or other commodities, nor should it attempt direct control of labour.

State planning of forms—Yes ; state planning and control of the economic process—No ! The essential thing is to recognize the difference between form and process, and to act accordingly.